contemporary

decoupage

An acrylic cylinder is the body of this lamp. Wrapping paper flowers are adhered to the underside and the background is filled in with a gold pearlized finish backed with orange acrylic paint.

This game table is large enough to seat six around it. The top, created by the author, is made of stamped metallic pieces and colored paper squares. The finish is urethane. The tabletop tilts to reveal a seat with a bench lid that covers a storage bin. Jane Bearman designed and executed the cut-paper card-queen. The entire design is buried in urethane.

A magazine advertisement is fragmented into thin strips to fit onto an acrylic-coated, expanded styrene foam egg.

contemporary decoupage

new plastic materials
new and traditional processes

THELMA R. NEWMAN

CROWN PUBLISHERS, INC., NEW YORK

To Eva F. Schnitzer

© 1972 by Thelma R. Newman

All rights reserved. No part of this book may be reproduced or utilized in any form or by any means, electronic or mechanical, including photocopying, recording, or by any information storage and retrieval system, without permission in writing from the Publisher.

Inquiries should be addressed to Crown Publishers, Inc., 419 Park Avenue South, New York, N.Y. 10016.

Library of Congress Catalog Card Number: 72-84321

ISBN: 0-517-500906
ISBN: 0-517-500914

Printed in the United States of America
Published simultaneously in Canada by
General Publishing Company Limited
Design: Nedda Balter and Ruth Smerechniak

acknowledgments

A resource book such as *Contemporary Decoupage* owes its existence to all those who preceded me in communicating about decoupage, and to those very special people who contributed their time and efforts to make this book possible. They are specially noted in caption credits.

Extraordinary thanks goes to Jane Bearman, Gini Merrill, Lydia Irwin, Lee Walker, Marie Mitchell, June Meier, Fran Willner, Fran Cohen, Dee Davis, and Dee Frenkel. And to Norm Smith who meticulously processed my photographs, I am extremely grateful for a beautiful job.

Most of all, continuing thanks go to my husband Jack and my son Lee, my models, and to my son Jay who helped in researching decoupage in Europe; their ever-present support is deeply appreciated.

All photographs and project designs by the author, unless otherwise noted.

contents

preface

There are few arts and crafts that so easily can produce such outstanding results. That is what captivates.

Whether decoupage is an art or craft depends upon one's emphasis. If imitation and reiteration are the code, and craftsmanship is of a high level, then decoupage is a craft. But if design is expressed in a significant way and given new meaning, then decoupage is an art. An ordinary object is transformed into an important communication through art. The latter is the emphasis I hoped to achieve in *Contemporary Decoupage*.

Some license is taken, a spin-off from the endless repetition of authorities by authorities. I hope that the new directions stimulated here find avenues of creative endeavor. Just as collage was once a threat to the approved forms of traditional painting and sculpture, so new decoupage can be a threat to a narrow interpretation of the art. It need not be so. Boundaries are moveable and should be moved.

I did not abandon traditional approaches. They weave throughout the book. Although license with process is taken, the greatest innovation is through use of uncommon materials and designs.

High design standards are important and maintained throughout. So much that has passed as decoupage is banal and ugly. For the quantities produced, little stands out as significant. Decoupage, though, has within its compass the potential to move out of the drawing room into the realm of significant expression with objects. I hope that the chapter on design and the projects featured are indicators of new possibilities.

Importantly, I think there needs to be an understanding of what materials can do. I am prejudiced against materials that are used as imitators, although I will admit that there are exceptions here. Nevertheless, I like to see wood used as wood, metal as metal, and paper as paper. And I do not like to see beautiful shapes decorated mainly because decoupage is a decorating process. Some objects should not be adorned; others cry out for some way to transport them to more important levels. I hope *Contemporary Decoupage* communicates this by example.

My point of view is not the only one represented within this book. I took a cross-country look at the creative output of decoupeurs. Their work is amply projected.

There have been some excellent books written by experts about decoupage, but almost without exception, these experts have had their own decoupage supply businesses. Often their description of materials is by trade names. I have no such affiliation. Even though I have indicated brand names, for expediency, in every case the generic material is mentioned. I have tried to bring my knowledge of plastics technology to *Contemporary Decoupage*, because in practice, almost all varnishes are a form of plastic and many plastics can be used as objects. I hope that the expansive chart on varnishes will summarize and illustrate for the reader the vast amount of coatings available. All varnishes that were used in over 40 projects have their advantages and disadvantages. It is only through exploration that one can find personal favorites for particular processes.

If *Contemporary Decoupage* fulfills my highest goals, it will inspire you to express your unique self, creatively.

T.R.N.

1

decoupage: its traditions and definitions

A Bit of History

Decoupage is a paper art and a French word meaning literally "a cutting out." Although decoupage is acknowledged to harken back to the 17th century, paper cutouts are as old as paper itself and the Chinese culture that invented paper. As a popular folk art, paper cutouts are almost as old as paper's introduction to Europe in the 12th and 13th centuries. Paper cutout tradition still persists in Poland, Yugoslavia, Rumania, Germany, Switzerland, in Mexico, the rest of the Americas, and nearly everywhere else in some form or other.

The specific style of decoupage of the 17th century—precise paper cutting from engravings that were hand-colored, glued, varnished, and finely sanded—was stimulated, ironically, by Chinese design. History tells us that Chinese lacquerware furniture was in short supply and high demand. Lacquerware became a status symbol. Venetian cabinetmakers sought a creative solution and designed cabinets that simulated Chinese lacquerware less expensively than it had cost to import. Thus emerged decoupage, called by the Italians *arte povero* or *lacche povero*, in a derogatory way, the poor man's art or lacquer. Few examples exist today because the work was done on inexpensive wood and, for the most part, did not hold up. Nevertheless, Venetian decoupage was ornamental, colorful, and opulent. Gesso was often used on backgrounds as a solution to cover the soft, uninteresting woods.

The art spread to France as *l'art scriban* with lacy cuttings, dainty flowers, cherubs, scenes, and butterflies predominating. En-

A 17th-century Italian decoupage using elements of hand-colored prints and hand-painting on a gesso background. Courtesy: Museo Civico, Padua, Italy.

A close-up of a side panel.

A close-up of the other side panel of the secretary.

A late 17th-century Italian chest with decoupage.
Courtesy: Museo Civico, Padua, Italy.

One side of the chest. Note the watercolored engravings and the painted finish over gesso.

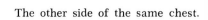

The other side of the same chest.

Drawers from a chest showing details of decoupage. Note the "chinoiserie" subject matter in the upper right-hand drawer. All other subject matter content reveals scenes from the life-style of the period. Courtesy: Museo Civico, Padua, Italy.

Another series of drawers from the same 17th-century Italian chest. On the upper drawer on the left, note the incongruous Oriental figure running into the background that does not relate to the subject matter of the rest of the drawers. Hand-colored engravings were used here, too, adhered to a gesso background.

gravings, etching, lithographs, block prints, and so on, reproduced art work by François Boucher, Jean-Antoine Watteau, and Jean-Baptiste Pillement. Pillement was famous for his chinoiserie—dancing Chinese figures, bridges, and exotic trees. In Germany and Austria, the influence was seen in Biedermeier style, with heavy designs incorporating embossed flowers and figures. In England, decoupage, called *japanning*, was translated into feathery, intricate design utilizing colored fine papers.

Decoupage styles paralleled the baroque and classic modes predominating in the 17th century, rococo in the 18th century, and Biedermeier influences in the 19th century. In Victorian England, Biedermeier was interpreted further into three dimensions until it evolved away from decoupage of the early form, emerging as a three-dimensional paper art.

Famous men, women, and families, working together from the 18th century onward, found decoupage entertaining and rewarding. Marie Antoinette made *découpure* pieces which were lacy outouts. Lord Byron and Beau Brummel are credited with having created large decoupage pieces. Mary Delany,

a member of a proud upper-class family in England, at the age of 74 (in 1774) made "paper mosaics," although not decoupage in an orthodox sense, working until 1784. Three years later when she died, she left a legacy of a thousand fantastically intricate paper flowers cut from hand-watercolored paper.

Blossoms without perfume that neither grew
   nor faded.
The rose that cannot wither . . .
                —Henry Vaughn in tribute
                   to Mary Delany

In the United States, Caroline Duer began working in decoupage interpreting a Biedermeier style in the early 1900s and had an exhibition of decoupage at the Addison Gallery in Andover, Massachusetts, in 1957 Also Maybelle and her son Hiram Manning brought the art back from France and conducted workshops that spawned many proponents. Carl Federer has created decoupage pieces for more than 25 years. And Marie Mitchell, Frances Wing, Dorothy Harrower, Patricia Nimocks, and Lee Walker are but a few of those who served to popularize decoupage in its traditional form in the past 30 years.

When gesso was used as a background, it often chipped and peeled away. Note the use of engravings in the trees and figures. This panel probably dates back to the early 18th century. Courtesy: Cooper-Hewitt Museum of Design, Smithsonian Institution, New York.

A very fine example of a Venetian, early-18th-century secretary. It is decorated in lacquer and the applied engravings are painted in a full range of colors and gold. Courtesy: The Metropolitan Museum of Art, New York, Fletcher Fund, 1925.

Some Definitions

Sprinkled throughout the history of paper art are variations on the theme of decoupage. What decoupage means is variously interpreted. One school of thought proposes that decoupage is the employment of reproductions in a new way, as cutouts that are pasted, varnished, and sanded until the original decoration is embedded and all one's fingertips can feel is smooth varnish. I prefer to consider this a valid definition of "traditional" decoupage.

There are other variations. Why not take liberties with any aspect of decoupage and carry it along a contemporary route as an art form? Dorothy Harrower defines decoupage as "representative, embodying cutouts that are redesigned to depict a scene, to re-create a period, to tell a story or to decorate a plain surface." Granted! Decoupage uses cut paper, as painting utilizes paint. Even though traditional painting once was a means to describe a life style, a story, to reflect man's image of God and religion, painting cannot be defined that way today. Nor should decoupage be circumscribed to past interpretation.

Scope and Potential

Decoupage has a broader scope and potential than reiteration of prescribed historical modes and media.

This German silhouette, circa 1800, in black paper on silk with lettering in ink, is a memorial to Hermann Billing. Cut paper was commonly used for memorial designs and crests. Courtesy: Cooper-Hewitt Museum of Design, Smithsonian Institution, New York.

Folk art employed all kinds of materials —fabric, cut paper, watercolor—so does collage. This Austrian example dates back to around 1760. Salome is receiving the head of John the Baptist from the executioner. Note that the heads, arms, legs, sword, bowl, and parts of the building and scenery are watercolor on cutout paper. Courtesy: Cooper-Hewitt Museum of Design, Smithsonian Institution, New York.

Another folk art example from South Germany (about 1820) that utilized fabric for the clothing and cutout watercolor for the body elements, the chickens, basket, knife, and walking stick. Courtesy: Cooper-Hewitt Museum of Design, Smithsonian Institution, New York.

One of Mary Delany's thousand cut paper flowers. Note that the precise detail is water-colored and then cut and pasted. Courtesy: The British Museum, London.

Another of Mrs. Delany's cut paper flowers. Courtesy: Cooper-Hewitt Museum of Design, Smithsonian Institution, New York.

Once collage was treated as a threat to painting because it encompassed a new dimension: it incorporated real materials into paintings. It was a shortcut that eliminated the need to reproduce textures with paint. But that was in the early 20th century. In 50 years, it became accepted as another means of expression. Collage concepts can open new avenues in decoupage design and subject matter, and lead to a more creative form of decoupage.

Along the way, various schools of art interpreted the collage in diverse ways. The Cubists, Surrealists, the Futurists, and others had their own way of using elements to articulate space. By the 20th century, parts of the collage composition were slipped behind one another in a hide-and-seek relationship, disappearing and reemerging in an interweaving of shapes.

From collage there emerged the photomontage, which juxtaposed planes consisting mainly of photographs or other reproductions into a composition, advertisement, film, and the like.

Collage and montage are assembled pasteups. So is decoupage. All three employ the cutting of some configuration, not necessarily created by the artist. All three involve an assemblage of elements not originally intended to be combined. All three can use components that incorporate the real thing without imitating it by painting the idea of the real thing. With such great similarities, the distinction among these forms of art can be ambiguous, particularly from a contemporary vantage point. If forced to determine the difference, let us say that decoupage means *cutting out, assembling flat materials, pasting up, and varnishing the whole*—whereas montage means cutting out, assembling flat materials, pasting up, but *not* varnishing. Collage, then, uses dissimilar materials, sometimes flat, sometimes incorporating painted components, pasting up, but not embedding forms in varnish. Collage most often is a fine art expression. Montage is usually employed in advertising, book design, and film-making. Decoupage is most often associated with three-dimensional useful forms, but not always.

Let us not draw fences around these distinctions. Let us incorporate the creative possibilities of all these forms and call it *Contemporary Decoupage.* Let us combine painted elements with paper cutouts (there is a tradition for this in early Venetian decoupage). Let us overlap planes if we find that our expression and interpretation of an object works better that way. Let us combine dissimilar materials and not confine our elements to paper (Victorians did this). Let us also extend beyond the two-dimensional and work in relief.

As we can see, liberation from the dominating traditions of the 18th and 19th century can lead to new vistas in subject matter and to use of new paints and varnishes. Pop art, for example, is one approach that can open us up to new images.

In the end, what we create in contemporary decoupage cannot be explained by orthodox interpretation. An art form that imitates yesterday's styles is not a valid expression for today. Our way of looking at things is different. Our environment is not the same. Our styles of dressing and our modes of living are unlike the past. There are images of today that belong to us—the poster, billboard, masses of printed materials, photographs, movies, and so on. Granted that some of yesterday's art forms hold a nostalgia and a beauty that we may want to recapture, but consider that today there are beautiful objects as well.

No matter how selective one is in producing a re-creation of a 18th- or 19th-century style, it still is not authentic and cannot be, because today's interpreter does not feel and see as yesterday's counterpart did. No original traditional form made *today* can be genuinely representative of decoupage tradition unless it is an exact imitation. Imitation is repetition. Moving ahead to reflect the present is a sign of vitality and life. Let us incorporate our heritage in what we do and also let us look to *today's* world, utilize its images and the best of what our technology will proffer. Then we will create an art form that, with the skills of the decoupage craft, will truly reflect our personal way of seeing.

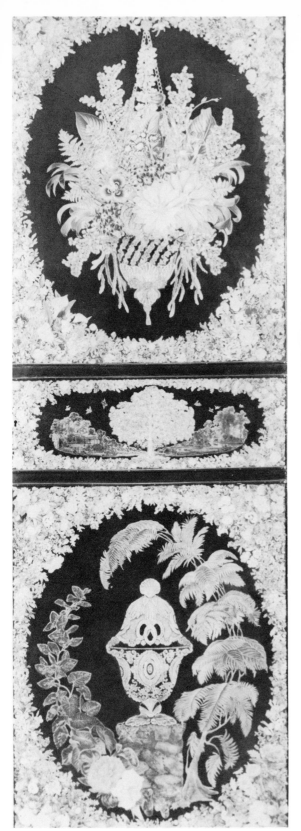

Carl Federer has worked in decoupage for at least 25 years. This is one of his decoupage panels called *Still Life with Bee and Cauliflower*. He used reproductions that were carefully cut and combined, with a sense of drama, into a composition.

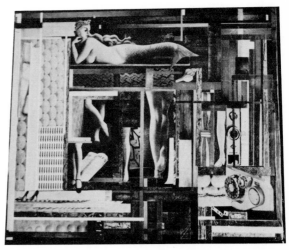

Another of Carl Federer's works called *Wistful Mermaid* (collection of August John Burkard) is as close to a montage as a decoupage, but it is varnished.

A door panel for a wardrobe by Caroline King Duer (circa 1935). She used German embossed flowers, leaves, and gold elements along with hand-colored printed materials. The total effect is very elegant.

Max Ernst used engravings from picture books, cut and pasted them into the incongruous collage entitled *Kindness Week or the Seven Capital Elements*. Courtesy: The Museum of Modern Art, New York.

Another of Max Ernst's collages of the same series. Courtesy: The Museum of Modern Art, New York.

In 1918, Kurt Schwitters created this collage (*Drawing R2 Hansi Schokolade*) of colored papers and wrappers. He called these compositions *merzbild*, literally meaning "garbage pictures." Courtesy: The Museum of Modern Art, New York.

Merz Drawing (Merzzeichnung) 1924, Kurt Schwitters. Made of pasted papers and a button. Courtesy: The Museum of Modern Art.

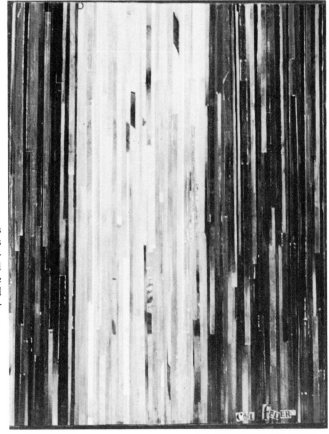

Carl Federer's *Dark Curtain* is
a fragmentation. He cuts strips
from pictorial elements and in-
terpolates them into a unified
piece. Note that even his name
is pieced together from printed
letters. For more on fragmentation, see Chapter 10.

Pablo Picasso, *Man with a Hat*.
(December 1912). Charcoal,
ink, and pasted paper were
combined into this collage.
Courtesy: The Museum of
Modern Art, New York.

Carlo Carra's *Patriotic Celebration* (1914) is a collage of printed words with painting over it. Courtesy: Dr. Gianni Mattioli, Milan, Italy.

Henri Matisse fused painting and sculpture into a technique known variously as cutouts, *papier collé gouaches découpées,* or collage. Matisse literally put down his brush and took up scissors. "Carving into color," Matisse called his new method. He often prepared his own colors on watercolor paper, too. In the direct cutout technique, color becomes at once the shape, surface, and contour. This is an early cutout pasted on canvas, called *Memory of Oceania* (1953). 9′4″ x 9′4⅞″. Courtesy: The Museum of Modern Art, New York.

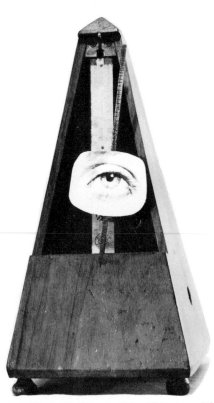

Man Ray's *Indestructible Object* or *Object to Be Destroyed* (1964) is a metronome with a cutout photograph of an eye on its pendulum. This Pop Art piece is a fine art expression—but why cannot it be called "decoupage"? Courtesy: The Museum of Modern Art, New York.

Jean Arp in *Collage with Squares Arranged According to the Law of Chance* (1916-17) watercolored the background and used colored papers. Courtesy: The Museum of Modern Art, New York.

One of Jane Bearman's compositions showing more distinctly the separation of various colors and textures. The dark shapes do not overlap, but are juxtaposed, as in decoupage.

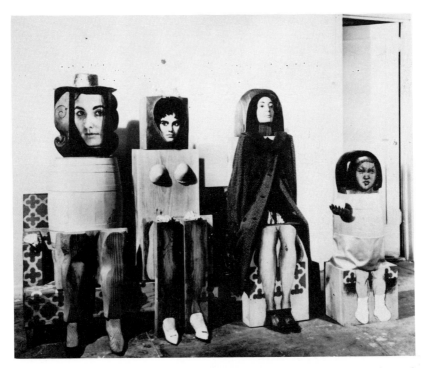

Marisol's *The Visit* is of mixed media in three dimensions, a sculptural form that among other materials utilizes reproductions, cut paper, and paint. Courtesy: Sidney Janis Gallery, New York. From the Dr. Peter Ludwig Collection, Wallraf-Richartz Museum, Cologne, Germany.

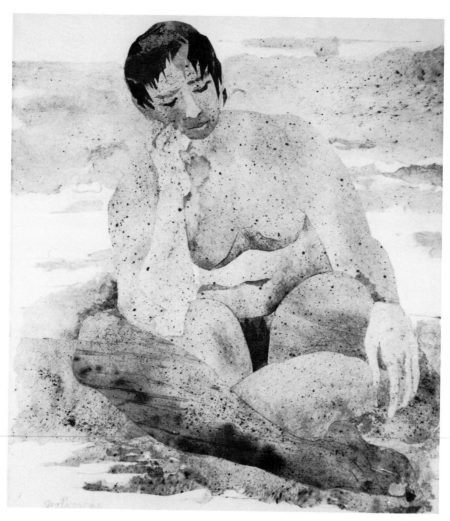

Jane Bearman used hand-colored papers of various textures, cut them into shapes and overlayed them into this composition of a woman. There is an acrylic emulsion coating over the entire piece. Jane Bearman calls this a painting. The distinction as to what label to use is not very clear. Need it be?

2

the language of decoupage design

Decoupage as Art

Decoupage, like other art forms, is successful if the artist communicates ideas creatively and uniquely and if he expresses them with skill and craftsmanship. The artist needs to know the meaning of the craft: what the materials can do, what its potential and limitations are, how one utilizes the language of design to communicate in decoupage form. A piece is successful only if all aspects are fulfilled.

The Decoupage Mode

What is uniquely decoupage? Flat pieces of paper are used to decorate a three-dimensional form. Scissors cut and tailor reproductions or textured and colored papers into shapes that are applied to three-dimensional objects, usually useful forms, such as cabinets, tables, boxes, doors, clocks, screens, and panels, to name a few. The edges of shapes are usually hard or crisp because that is the way a scissors cuts. (If paper is torn, the edge is soft and, when glued, blends into the background.) The paper, then, is adhered in a designed arrangement, flat or in relief. The entire piece is then coated with many layers of a transparent varnish, with sanding at different stages and reapplication of varnish until the edges of the paper disappear into the varnish and one cannot feel the perimeters of the paper shapes any longer. Then paper design and object, through glue and varnish, are wed into an integral whole. The shape of the form and its decoration become one. Design transforms the object into something else, something that did not exist before. That is the "magic" of decoupage. With a minimum commitment to mastering the skill, and a maximum adherence to good design principles, a new form emerges, and the entirely new object is yours.

The uniqueness, the creativeness, and ultimately the success of your decoupage form depend upon the effectiveness of your design. Of course skill is important. Competence in decoupage technique is not difficult to acquire—a bit of practice and you will have the technical proficiency to be a master. Craftsmanship, however, is not enough to guarantee a quality piece. Commitment and sensitivity to good design, in my opinion, come first. Intuition is bolstered with exposure to well-designed objects and with much practice at seeing and doing. Good design is difficult to define, yet concepts of good design imply quality and have not changed over the ages.

Although some styles have traditions that lock the designer into what should or should not be done, for example, a formal balance for Empire period design, contemporary design knows no bounds and the de-signer is free to utilize the best of tradition and invent new and personal solutions.

General Design Concepts in Brief

The creative elements utilized in designing are materials, the symbol-tools of expression, and the unity of the whole. In decoupage, materials are basically papers, scissors, glues, paints and varnishes, sandpapers and waxes. Knowing how to use a scissors, glue, and so on are very important for a craftsmanlike result. Symbol-tools are the way we manipulate elements and concepts of design as a language to express an idea. For example, lines can be peaceful (horizontal) frantic (jagged and diagonal); shapes can be encompassing (a circle in a circle), or electric (a diagonal lightning form).

Decoupage is *applied design*. Applied design can bestow further richness to a form, such as a series of concentric circles around a drawer pull. It should, above all, suit the material and shape. When thoughtfully conceived, applied designs can enhance and strengthen the visual qualities of an object. Design should be so integral that it seems inseparable; the object could not be conceived of without that particular application.

This arrangement is not terrible, but the chicken design seems a bit too overpowering for the plate size.

The proportion of background to design is better here, using a larger tray.

The proportion of this picture to the background plate is poor because the piece is too solid and confined. If the plate were twice the size or very much smaller, the effect would be better. As it is now, the proportions are too much the same.

Here is another version, far better in proportion to the plate size. The plate becomes the design, with its wooden structure as background serving just as a defining frame.

DESIGN VARIABLES

Color, with its concomitants, dark and light, repetition of shape size and direction, size and grouping (mass), interval and density, are variable elements relating to material. For instance, what is the hue (name of the color), value (darkness or lightness), and intensity (strength of hue) of the shape to be used? How are the elements of the design to be grouped? Will they be small repeating units, clustered together, or arranged in a spiral direction? What rhythms will be created by your shapes if you group in twos and threes and leave small spaces between design elements—or permit large spaces between repeating forms? How do you iterate colors, directions, sizes—or is every aspect of your design disparate, unlike any other? Does it hold together, can the eye follow these elements?

DESIGN MEANS

Design *means* relate to design *variables*. In fact, some means and variables are one and the same. To make a distinction, however, design *means* are elements relating to space—how we express ourselves, the symbols we employ: texture, color, line, planes, shapes and balance of shapes, and darks and lights in a given space.

Are we relating the surface of the object to the surface of our applied paper? Is the paper texture one we can feel tactilely or visually? Are there repeating patterns, such as waves, or leaves on a tree that create texture effects? Is our background another texture, such as heavily grained wood? Does this wood pattern complement the leaf pattern or is there too much happening, too much to look at? If we are working on a vertical cylinder vase, should the design spiral or be applied in concentric rings? How will the shapes work best on a given form so that the grouping of these design elements creates a rhythm and direction for the eye to follow? Do we achieve a dynamic effect if we place a shape in the center of a large flat shape, or is the relationship of design to space better enhanced when we place our object to one side, to balance informally, so that planes of space around the object have more variety?

Squint at your arrangement so you can see dark and light relationships (without associating surface detail and color). Is the relationship between dark and light too evenly distributed? Would it be better to group or mass some elements? Do the values of dark and light balance—formally or informally? Would another organization of darks and lights provide more satisfying variety?

Balance can help to determine whether a piece will have a dynamic impact or be deadly dull. With these fish placed in a formal balance at the center of the plate, areas are evenly divided. Although formal balance is acceptable, this arrangement can be vastly improved by changing the symmetrical organization.

Balancing the fish informally is a much more successful and dynamic arrangement.

The formal spacing of these identical flowers, with almost equal amounts of background area all around, produces a static result.

Cutting away some leaves and arranging the flower elements in a diagonal line, with informal balance, we are more in keeping with the Oriental theme that the object and design suggest. Print by Patricia Nimocks.

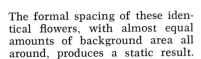

Here is another interpretation of these same flowers with more leaves cut away and the flowers joined at the pencil point. Again, the arrangement is a modified diagonal—an informal or asymmetrical spatial organization.

The problem here is fitting two similar floral forms onto this mirror.

By cutting away some floral elements, the bouquets seem to be continuous. The balance is informal.

DESIGN ORGANIZATION

All design elements relate part-to-part and parts-to-the-whole. Similarity of elements to one another, unity of elements or variety, positives (the shapes) and negatives (the spaces around the shapes), rhythm (continuity and variations of the elements), contrasts of size, texture, form, darks and lights, direction (horizontal, vertical, diagonal, or calm, elevating, active) are all design organization factors.

Is the size of the applied piece dominating the object? Is it in scale? Are there negative spaces that are smaller in size? Do they add some variety and repetition that give direction to the eye? Do all shapes have the same basic contour or are there some variations of the contours? What new shapes are created in the background as one shape is placed in proximity to another? Are you combining straight lines with curved lines? How do these relate to or repeat the contours of your object? Does the major direction of placement of your elements reflect a dominant feeling—peacefulness for horizontal ordering, for example; similarly, does the shape (or subject matter) evoke a feeling? Is the position of elements end-to-end, parallel, diagonal, overlapping, superimposed, intersecting, interpenetrating, accidental, sequential, closed, detached? Does the form and its relationship to other forms imply direction such as up, down, side to side, slanting, advancing or receding, over and under, radiating, concentric, spiraling?

Color Combinations

Colors can be combined in many ways. There are no hard and fast rules as to which colors go best because there are too many exceptions. Of all the combinations, monochromatic and complementary color harmonies are the most traditional. A look to nature will eliminate all prejudices because nature's harmonies know no bounds and are endless.

MONOCHROMATIC COLORS

One color dominates and is the only color used. Variations are made with tints (mixing with water to dilute color or white to lighten color), tones (adding black), and variations of the darkness of color between the tints and tones.

COMPLEMENTARY COLORS

Complementary colors are those opposite one another on the color wheel: red and green, blue and orange, yellow and violet. To dull a color, add a *bit* of its complement. To enchance and brighten (or vibrate) a color, place complements of the same hue, value, and intensity side by side.

TRIADIC COLORS

Triadic harmonies are three colors equidistant on the color wheel, such as red, yellow, and blue or green, orange, and violet. These may be modified by adding neutrals such as black and white.

RELATING COLORS

All colors can be made to relate by using a common denominator color. For example, if you wish red, blue, gray, and orange to relate, mix a small amount of the red into the blue, gray, and orange—or use any other of these colors as a common color, instead.

ANALOGOUS COLORS

Colors that sit next to one another on the color wheel relate and generally go well together. For example, red-violet, violet, and blue-violet relate; or yellow, yellow-green, and green go together.

WARM AND COOL COLORS

Colors such as red, orange, and yellow are warm, whereas blue and green are considered cool. When distributed in a design, contrast between warms and cools is often strong enough not to warrant change of value (darkness and lightness). Warm colors can be made cooler and the converse is true as well. For instance, to cool off a red, add a bit of blue or a bit of its complement, green.

LIMITING COLORS

It is best not to use every color in a design but to limit your palette. Selection of a particular palette can have a great range of choice. For instance, use blacks, grays, and whites; or earth colors such as browns, ochres, terra-cottas, and grays; high-key and low-key combinations where most colors have similar values. High-key combinations would be predominantly light in value while low-key elements would be mainly dark.

Limiting color to a monochromatic variation or analogous or complementary palette are valid delimitations; but selecting a palette, on the other hand, because the subject matter dictates it is *not valid*. It is too restricting and can be deadly dull. Selection of a color should satisfy likes and dislikes, mood, and design parameters. Only the beginner feels constrained to use colors dictated by a subject.

DOMINANCE, SUBORDINATION, ACCENT

The beginner might wisely follow this old rule based on dominance, subordination, and accent. Allow one color to dominate, use a second color in a subordinate role, and a third color (or colors) for accent. Modify color values to balance darks and lights. After you have followed this rule, break it and look for other solutions.

Design Motifs and Subject Matter

Designs can be inspired by or derived from many sources—materials, organization, and subject matter. Often all three work together to produce a final unified design.

Materials offer a great range of design possibilities—colors, values, textures of various kinds. A new treatment for a material can suggest a design or a special color may be exciting enough to use as a focal point.

Shapes of various kinds of objects can inspire—such as geometric motifs, dots, circles, checks, stripes.

Forms of nature, man-made objects, reproductions from books, magazines, prints, forms of your environment such as playing cards and labels, and the rich inspiration of nature such as leaves and rocks can be used. The best subject matter is usually found nearby, something with which you are familiar.

Learn to see perceptively. Open your vision to everything. Then analyze subjects for line, contour, color, texture, value. Use these stimuli as a springboard for a design motif. Play around with different relationships of just a few elements. Do not be afraid to snip and change the original subject matter context. Play up or down qualities. Change relationships. Try combining the seemingly incongruous. Take license with your scissors. Cut away and combine.

REPRESENTATIONAL, ABSTRACT, NON-OBJECTIVE

Subject matter may faithfully try to represent nature as the camera could mirror it or as an artist would interpret from the real world. Abstraction derives from nature but does not try to emulate it. The degree of abstracting can vary as much as a person's private way of seeing will allow. License is taken with shapes, colors, and textures. Non-objective art is non-representational; it is pure shape and color, knowing no direct relationship to the read world. It can be purely geometric design or be relationships of lines in space, or colored shapes to one another, to indicate a few possibilities.

All these styles have application to decoupage. The most valid are those abstract and non-objective designs that are two-dimensional in quality and do not attempt to pierce the flat surface of an object with illusions of perspective. There are exceptions, of course; *trompe l'oeil* deliberately plays with perspective and detail to give illusion of tactile and spatial qualities to a composition. Generally, though, good applied design is the skin of a surface and does not dig into it through depth-penetrating illusions.

The problem here is fitting a flat form into a concavity—the inside of this papier-mâché bowl.

To solve the problem, all appendages are cut away so that they can be completely rearranged to fit. Smaller pieces fit curves better than larger solids.

Some elements are eliminated, others are shortened and still others are placed in a different position than in the original. They are temporarily held in place with a plastic putty called Plasti-Tak.

Design Organization

Some people have a completed design in their minds before they begin. Another way to work is from drawings or plans. And another is to start with a spark, a nucleus of an idea and then manipulate parts directly on the object, arranging and rearranging the various elements of your design.

Once the materials and motifs have been selected and the function of the object has been considered, you are ready to organize your design. Two important considerations should be maintained throughout the creative process: they are the part-to-part and the part-to-whole relationships. The part-to-part relationship considers the way parts of the design relate in terms of color, shapes, lines, textures, negative and positive spaces; how they work together to create a continuity and wholeness. The part-to-whole relationship is by no means separate but relates to how well all the design works with the whole object. Any part of the design that "makes no difference" to the whole should be removed. Even if the design functions well as a design, if it does not relate to the color,

texture, shape, and function of the form, then try for another solution. Do not hold to a design idea as if that design *must* be used; save it for something else if it does not work!

As the eye moves around the object's shape from element to element, consider relationships of sizes, colors, textures, spaces and shapes, and the continuity of the design. Every shape has its own requirements. A cube demands a different treatment from a sphere. Look at museum-quality objects and notice the solutions of design to shape.

Consider, also, that your design elements were once two-dimensional. They probably came from books, magazines, prints—all sheets of paper. You are now transposing this two-dimensional shape onto three dimensions. Whereas, in a two-dimensional design, all parts are visible at once, on a three-dimensional shape only some parts can be seen at any one time, such as the one-third of a design that can be seen on a cylinder at one time, unless it is transparent. Yet each part must relate to the next and maintain a continuity. The "back" should not be treated any less importantly than the "front."

Given reversible colored paper (a different color on each side) and a standard-size wooden serving tray, the possibilities for design are endless. Setting a theme, such as folk art forms, delimits somewhat. Then restraining subject matter to one flower element repeated in three sizes, one bird, and leaf-stem units repeated in different sizes, we can start to play around with arrangements. This arrangement is formal and considers only one color.

Another factor is introduced, that of color. Here is a variation of the first arrangement showing contrast of some units.

Most of the second color becomes predominant with a grouping of the first color within a confined area which is framed by the second color.

A different element is introduced. It does not work because it distracts from the design continuity, acting like arrows that point out of the design area.

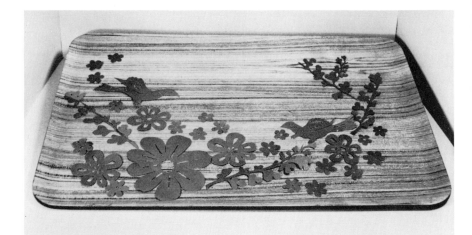

Most of the same elements are retained in an informally balanced design, again using just one color.

A second color is introduced here. The arrangement seems to have some superfluous elements on the right side.

The final solution finds some more manipulation of units necessary, eliminating some elements and permitting one color to dominate. If the design were only of flowers, the subject matter would not "say" as much as when the bird was introduced. The bird establishes a center of interest and directs the eye along the line of direction of the whole design, until one looks at the very last blossom.

UNITY AND VARIETY

Without unity of elements, no design exists, no matter how interesting the parts. It is a hodge-podge instead. Similarly, without variety, the result is boring and dull.

Unity is achieved by a sense of "rightness" in utilizing the design concepts mentioned earlier. Unity is a harmonious relationship of shape, color, line, value, texture, and so on. Repetition of any of these elements is an almost certain way of achieving unity. Relating the design direction to the contour of the form you are working on is another vital way to achieve unity.

Variety does not imply varying every element. It may mean reducing the number of elements and working for subtle changes within the scope of thickness, texture, value, or hue. Do not seek elaborate solutions to achieve variety, try for simple means.

Severe limitations, in fact, usually beget better design than an overabundance of possibilities. An understated design is also better than too much to look at, an overcrowding of a surface. Background space is important—no less important than pauses in music.

Starting with a single element, how many variations can you design into it using scissors only?

Four distinct shapes emerged from the original star form in the upper left of the picture. The next choice is how many ways one can arrange these elements, repeating some, so that they become a unified design.

34

In Summary

Pay serious attention to the creative designing phase of the decoupage process. When planning, ask yourself the questions proposed earlier and consider factors of color and organization. No one can give you solutions or even set up a sure-fire formula. And there is no sequence that will insure success as in a step-by-step description of a technical process, because design is personal and immensely vast in possibility. Planning the design can be the most enjoyable part of any expression and produces almost as much satisfaction as finally admiring the finished piece.

Start with the silhouette of a real object. Depict it though cutting and respacing, using all the material. Try simplifying and abstracting until you reduce the form to the most essential elements. The negative spaces become delineating lines.

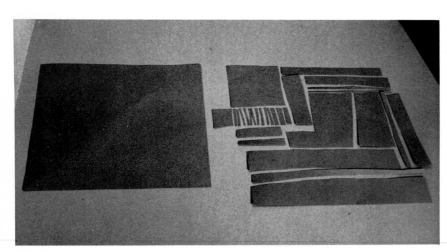

Starting with a rectangle, how many ways can you transform it, using only scissors? One approach is to slit the rectangle up into new forms that relate to one another but still retain the essential rectangular form. Movement is achieved by repeating small elements. Try these possibilities: use curved lines on each side; divide the shape with horizontal and vertical cuts; cut concentric curves around three circular areas like graining in wood; cut into only one side—and so on.

Start with a triangle. Cut new triangles and still maintain the integrity of the original equilateral triangle. Try changing the perimeter and regroup the pieces; modify the arrangement into a stretched out s shape, and so on.

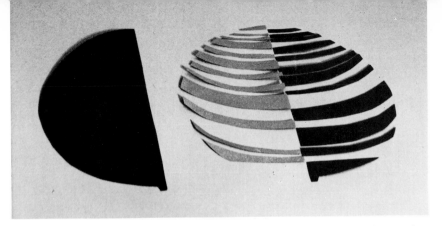

Start with half of a representational form, such as a leaf. Cut shapes that represent the internal ordering of the leaf, the veins. Fold back the design and you have counterchange. The negative spaces on one side of the axis become the positive shapes directly on the opposite side of the vertical stem. This also is an abstraction. Try folding back other shapes.

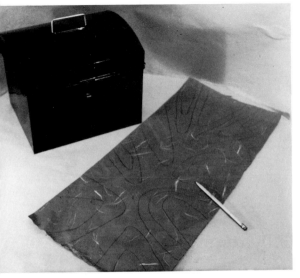

Given one tin box, Japanese textured paper, pencil, and scissors, create a design using all parts of the original paper.

The choice I favored was to draw a central axis, abstracting from a tree trunk, and then slicing repeating curves from all the sides of the original rectangle.

The central unifying form is tacked into place on the tin box. Note that the diagonals of the design repeat and that there is variety of size. This concept begins to transform an ordinary box into an attractive container. The usual decoration for this shape is a cliché using stars, flags, and eagle. See project "Cut Paper in Silhouette" in Chapter 9.

3

the traditional

decoupage process

Decoupage is an art that any interested person can learn. Once the skills are mastered and design becomes a high level consideration, the results are truly works of art. No drawing skill is needed. If one can color with pencils and fill in areas with watercolors, an added personal touch distinguishes and further individualizes the work. But even coloring skills are not necessary. If one can cut, paste, varnish, and sand, paying meticulous attention to precise technique, then a perfect product is assured. That is probably the reason that decoupage has become so popular nationally.

No other art experience is necessary, just time and patience. There is no danger of disappointment and the results are unique and precious. Just practice these basic, traditional skills. Do not skip or hurry over any step and mastery is yours. Variations of traditional approaches come later.

Sources for Decorations

Sources for decorations are all around us, thanks to the great variety of communication media. Once, the decoupeur only had prints to use—engravings, lithographs, block prints, and etchings. We have those and much more.

Paper prints are used in traditional decoupage. Thin paper stock is best, but there are ways to thin the paper if your print is too thick. Some sources are from old art books, or any other books, greeting cards, playing cards, magazines, calendars, Oriental prints and other art prints, wrapping paper, wallpaper, posters, coloring book pictures (printed on fine papers), portfolios, catalogs, and specially printed prints for decoupage. Bookstores, old and new print shops, and antique shops are great browsing places for surprise finds. Other avenues are listed in back of this book in the "Supply Sources" section.

Trims of gold and silver foil backed with paper are also used in Victorian and contemporary decoupage styles. These are available everywhere from department stores to arts and crafts stores. Often sources suggest a design theme. Other times a style or period will dictate the range of possibility and theme limitations. For Victorian decoupage, embossed prints work very well, but for the French styles of the 18th century, Pillement cupids and scenes as well as exotic flowers, garlands, and birds would be more appropriate.

Don't waste your time on cheap papers, prints that are reproduced poorly, or photostats and photos that will fade in time. Recoupage takes so much time and labor that it would be a pity to waste all that effort when the keystone of your work, the decoration, is cheap and temporary. You can, however, use a picture that has printing on the back, if at first you spray both sides with a clear acrylic sealer such as Krylon or Blair. If your print still shows through from the back, paint the back with white acrylic paint. Some aniline dyes bleed; check for that by spraying your print before spending your time cutting it. Black or brown printing on white or ecru paper is best for coloring. In fact, the traditional decoupeur values hand-colored work. Some avid decoupeurs buy expensive prints and then have them reproduced on appropriate papers. This allows for repetition of elements, but more importantly, does not destroy a precious original.

Thinning a Print

Prints on heavy paper can be used if you are willing to apply dozens of extra coats of varnish, or if in contemporary techniques, you do not embed the decorations. If you peel away excess paper, however, you can save a good deal of labor. This is optional.

Several approaches are recommended. One is to moisten the back of the print with white vinegar, enough to coat it, but not to saturate it. After letting the print sit for a few minutes, you can gently rub off the excess paper with your finger, or rub it with a slightly water-dampened sponge. After enough paper is removed, sponge off remaining vinegar with water. Let the print dry, then spray it with sealer.

Another method is to spray only the printed side with three thin coats of clear acrylic spray, to protect the color. Allow the coatings to dry between applications. When thoroughly dry, soak the print in slightly lukewarm water for about ten minutes. Then rub and peel away excess paper from the back. Marie Mitchell recommends sanding the back of the print with #280 sandpaper and detergent soap suds. Then rub the sudsy paper with your fingers in a circular motion until enough paper is removed. After the paper is dry you can smooth rough spots by sanding with #600 dry sandpaper.

Other authorities recommend scraping away paper with a razor blade or knife, but the risk of tearing the print is much greater with this method.

Selecting the Object

Theoretically, any object made of any material can be decoupaged. In actuality, some objects do not lend themselves to decoration. Their surface may be too exciting in texture or the design of the object may be so important that a decoration would be a distraction. Often modern designs fall into this category.

Objects to be decorated can range from trays, jewelry, purses, plates, vases, bowls, cups, boxes, plaques, and bookends to room accessories such as wastepaper baskets, doors, mirrors, lamps, screens, to furniture such as tables, bed headboards, cabinets, chests of drawers, desks, pianos, and the unusual such as shoes, protective helmets, and rocks—to name a few.

Matching Decoration to Object

Do some measuring. Study your print and your object. Play around with different possibilities of positioning your decorations. Try to think of alternatives—other prints, different ways of using them, even imagine doing some drastic surgery on your decora-

Design sources can be many—coloring books, posters, prints of various kinds, advertisements, specially prepared decoupage materials, and gold foil embossed trims, to name a few.

An assortment of objects made of wood. Some already have a color or finish.

Here are a few unfinished objects that have great decoupage possibilities. All these forms seem to "ask" for decoration.

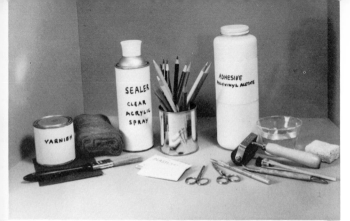

Some of the materials used in decoupage: Varnish, sandpaper, and brush on the left to sealer, colored oil pencils, Plasti-Tak in the center, and scissors, knife, burnisher, roller, sponge, water, and glue on the right.

Materials used solely for finishing the object: Stain and sealer, tack cloth, steel wool, waxes, brushes, sandpapers, Scotch-Brite.

Materials used mainly in coloring, cutting, and preparing the design to be used on the object.

Fancy paper and fabrics, marbled and printed, used in the lining and covering of boxes and drawers.

tion. Try combining different elements. Think of appropriate background colors and if you are to color your print, coordinate your colors. This is all preparatory to the next steps, which are coloring your print and preparing the surface of your object.

Coloring Your Print

You color only prints that are not already colored, unless, using acrylic paint, you wish to touch up an area, add an accent, change a color, or apply a shadow to an already colored piece.

Three materials are recommended: oil or watercolor pencils, watercolor, or acrylic paint diluted to watercolor consistency.

OIL AND WATERCOLOR PENCILS

Oil-based pencils provide richer values and tones than watercolor pencils. The technique with both, however, is the same. Derwent, Prismacolor, Venus, and Paradise are oil-based pencils. Mongol is water-based. When coloring you have many choices, filling in areas with even applications of bright and obvious color, as I did in the medieval print on the plate, or by observing highlights and shadows and rendering a realistic interpretation of color.

If you are using flat planes of color, then just apply color evenly as you did with crayons in your coloring book, a few years back.

If you wish to model your areas, start with your *lightest* value (with the lightest pressure on your pencil) first, and gradually work to your darkest values. Do not be afraid to use other colors in highlights and shadows. Let us say you are coloring a red apple. Do use some yellows and greens in the lighter areas and some blues and purples in the darker portions. Try for an even background overall coloring for the first application of color, add textures and details *after* the basic overlay of color has been applied. Keep your pencils finely sharpened. Remember that colors nearest to you are more intense and detailed than colors at a distance. Do not use

A black and white copy of a medieval print on watercolor paper from a Dover coloring book. Watercolor or diluted acrylic color can be used. Colors should be transparent and not opaque like gouache or tempera, otherwise the print outlines would be obliterated.

Colored oil pencils are excellent. Keep them sharp.

all your colors. Limit your palette. Try to stylize a design. For example, try combining yellow-ochre, terra-cotta, and brown in a design, or gray, white, and black in another. In fact, 18th-century design used one predominant color, terra-cotta, in all shadows (applied lightly), with the addition of light and dark greens for foliage and with just touches of blue, pink, red, flesh, yellow, and light yellow. Burnt carmine (a brownish red) was used for intensifying and accenting. With terra-cotta colored in every shadow, a unified color scheme was guaranteed. Another early 18th-century palette was *en grisaille*—which was predominantly gray monochrome reminiscent of marble sculpture with turquoise blue, terra-cotta, and opaque white also used.

WATERCOLOR AND WATER-THINNED ACRYLIC

Watercolor and water-thinned acrylic produce the same results. The only difference is that once acrylic dries, the color is permanent and cannot be lightened and sponged away as in a watercolor. Techniques for both are the same.

Employing watercolor rather than coloring with pencils is a good deal faster, results look freer, and colors can be more brilliant. As with pencils, and even more importantly for watercolor, start with lights and work gradually to dark areas. Apply details last. Colors dry differently on different papers. Try mixing various combinations of colors and practice color palettes on a piece of white watercolor paper first.

Do not use opaque colors such as gouache, which is watercolor with the addition of opaque white, tempera color, or very thickly applied acrylic. Their opacity obliterates print outlines and details.

Sealing the Print

Sealing your print is a simple but important step. Sealing keeps watercolor pencil and watercolor from smearing in the gluing operation. It contains color and keeps aniline dyes from bleeding and mottling. For prints, it prevents rubbing off of color as the surface of the print is sponged or pressed with your fingers.

Sealers also strengthen the paper and reinforce delicate cuttings and protect paper from discoloration by varnishes. Sealers plug a paper's porosity and prevent the penetration of other materials. Some sealers are applied by flowing the sealer over the print with a brush, blotting off excess with a paper towel; others are sprayed via a spray can. I prefer the spray-can sealers. Krylon and Blair are excellent and although they cannot be purchased through mail-order firms because of flammability codes, they are available in paint, arts and crafts supply, hardware, and in department stores. These are acrylic-based clear coatings, usually mat in texture, although some are glossy or glazed. The mat type is best, but the glazed variety works also and is particularly good for special projects.

Spray-seal your print with two light coats on each side, allowing a drying period of about three minutes between coats before cutting. However, some papers, such as coated papers, are too stiff and brittle for a pre-cutting spray. In that case, spray-seal after your design has been cut out.

Another seal material is shellac diluted with one-fourth alcohol into a thin material that is brushable.

Preparing Your Object

RAW WOOD

A new wooden form (without hinges and other hardware) needs to be sanded at first with #100 garnet paper. Joining-cracks and nail holes can be filled with a fine filler such as wood, vinyl, or acrylic modeling paste. A second sanding with #220 garnet paper readies the wood for dusting with tack cloth (a resinous varnish waxy-feeling cheesecloth) and then for staining or sealing.

For staining, if the wood is beautiful in grain and clear in finish, without mars and fillers, I like to use a water-soluble alcohol-based stain. Water-diluted acrylic works very well, too. Sponge or brush the stain onto the wood in the direction of the grain. Remove excess immediately with a soft absorbent rag. Be certain that the stain dries completely before applying anything else to the surface. Acrylic seals the grain and readies the wood for varnishing. After using a water-based stain, seal the wood with two coats of fresh shellac diluted one part shellac to one part denatured alcohol, or with a sealer such as WaterLox or with two coats of acrylic emulsion (polymer medium). Each application of sealer should dry thoroughly before a new coat is added.

If you are to paint the wood later with an oil-based paint, then seal the wood with two coats of shellac. Never use shellac over any other finish but raw wood. If you have doubts as to the compatibility of one coat over another and do not want to risk peeling and bubbling, then use a material such as McCloskey's Be-Tween-Kote which acts as an adhesive between coats. It actually glues the top coat to the foundation coat to prevent delamination. It also eliminates sanding for adhesion. It should be used only as a sandwich coat between epoxies, polyurethanes, enamels, and oil-based paints. Other commercial seals are also good. It is advisable to read labels on paint cans thoroughly to be assured of the compatibility of finishes.

If acrylic is used, it acts as a sealer as well as a color-coating vehicle. If the wood is open-grained, then two coats of acrylic probably would be necessary.

In summation, this axiom will help: Stain before sealing and seal before painting.

VARNISHED WOOD

Varnished wood should be washed with denatured alcohol to clean away foreign matter. If the varnish is shellac instead, then the alcohol will attack and help to remove the old shellac. If you wish to remove the old surface some more, sand with #100 garnet paper to provide surface "tooth" to hold further coatings. It is not necessary to expose the bare wood. Repair and fill in dents and cracks with vinyl filler or acrylic modeling paste, if necessary, and sand again. The wood is now ready for painting with acrylic or any other colorant vehicle.

PAINTED WOOD

If a piece has been well painted and there are no chips and bruises, it need only be sanded with #100 garnet paper. Chips in the paint can be rubbed out with #100 and #220 garnet paper. After sanding, wipe the piece with denatured alcohol to remove remaining foreign matter. If any area needs to be brought down to raw wood, proceed as if the wood in that area is a new surface. The piece should now be ready for painting. A slightly roughened surface will anchor acrylic, but if the water-based acrylic beads up and is repelled, then spray-seal the surface with a clear acrylic spray.

For badly painted wood, use a heavy-bodied paint remover following the directions on the can. Scrape away the old paint with a scraper, razor, or putty knife. Attack only a small area at a time. Sometimes the operation has to be repeated to completely remove the paint. When finished, wash the surface with denatured alcohol and when dry, sand with #100 garnet paper to even out roughness. Then complete the usual filling, sanding, and sealing. The surface should now be ready for painting.

ANY NEW METAL

Clean away protective oils on tin and other metals with denatured alcohol. A oil-based primer for metal prevents rusting and provides a base for painting. This has to dry overnight. Some paints for metal are rust-inhibiting. In that case, one or two coats are sufficient. These paints can provide protection for new metal and become your background color.

OLD METAL

Old metal which has been previously painted is prepared by removing paint with #60 garnet "Open-Cote" cabinet paper, wire brush, and scraper or with paint remover.

Emery cloth does a fine job of removing rust. For stubborn rust spots, use Rusticide or another rust remover. After removing the old paint, wipe down the piece with denatured alcohol, wipe away dust with a tack cloth, and apply your metal primer and paint. After the paint dries, sand away any specks with #400 wet-or-dry sandpaper.

CERAMIC, MARBLE, STONE, AND GLASS

Clean thoroughly with soap and water; then wipe with denatured alcohol. Spray acrylic or a mat urethane sealer onto the surface in two light coats. When the coatings dry thoroughly, you are ready to glue decorations into place.

APPLICATION OF GESSO

Traditionally, gesso was a mixture of bolted whiting, rabbitskin glue, and water. This mixture belongs to yesteryear because it does not pay to prepare gesso or use these inferior materials. They crack, shrink, and chip. Acrylic gesso is an excellent product and readily available.

Acrylic gesso, which is the consistency of sour cream, should be used directly on new rough wood, or over a sealer on glass. Its purpose is primarily to hide seams or interfering grain, and to provide a satin smooth finish.

Hiram Manning suggests opening the "pores" of the wood by applying one part clear ammonia and one part denatured alcohol mixed together in a pungent combination, to the wood, and allowing it to dry before applying the gesso. This is optional. What it is supposed to do is to allow the gesso to sink into the wood.

To apply acrylic gesso, use a stiff-bristle brush that had been dampened with water and is fully charged with gesso. Use light, rapid strokes, at first in one direction and then at right angles. Each coat is applied over the other as soon as the glossy surface becomes dull and mat-looking.

To smooth gesso, after it has dried al-

most hard, sand in a circular motion (light pressure) with #400 wet-or-dry sandpaper that has been dipped into water. If you have difficulty judging where remaining imperfections are, lightly rub charcoal over the surface and dust it off. Charcoal should linger in any indentations. After the gesso has dried thoroughly, wrap a piece of dampened china silk around your fingers and polish the gesso to a porcelain-like surface.

You are now ready to paint the surface. Since acrylic gesso was used, application of acrylic paint requires no surface preparation. Other paints can be used as well, if you wish, but first coat the surface with alcohol-diluted shellac.

Cutting

Every step in decoupage is important and should be carried out skillfully, but cutting is most important because what is cut is the substance of your design.

Precise cutting is usually accomplished with a fine steel, small scissors with curved blades that resembles a cuticle scissors or one that is used in eye surgery. Embroidery scissors, straight bladed and small, are also useful. Some people feel a knife is easier to handle. Generally, greater precision comes with a scissors cutting.

Scissors are held with the thumb and third (middle) finger in a relaxed manner with the curved blade pointing to the right and away from the edge being cut. Feed the object being cut into the scissors, with scissors opening and closing in a steady rhythm, but remaining essentially in the same position. The design is always held loosely on the left of the blade as you cut.

If the design is very large, divide it into units of about eight inches in diameter for easier manipulation. If you cut it at connecting points, the cut pieces will glue together without revealing the slice.

Generally, trim away excess paper from around the design. Next cut away interior spaces with scissors held underneath the paper, unless it is not possible to do so; and last, follow the contour of the shape, trim-

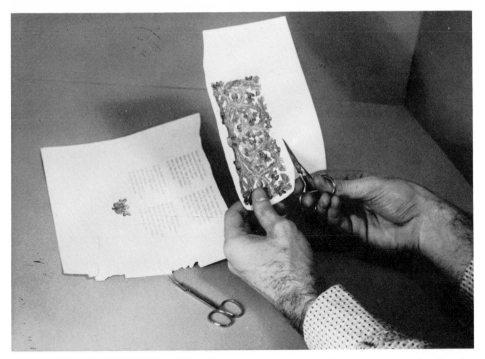

To cut your design, trim away excess paper. A straight-bladed scissors works fine for this process. This design came from an old Norwegian book found in a second-hand bookshop.

Next, from the back, holding the curve of the scissors away from the cutting edge, puncture a hole, insert the scissors, trim out interior spaces. With the left hand, feed the design into the scissors.

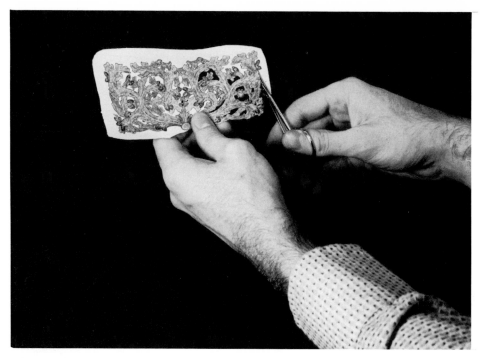

After all the interior spaces are cut away, trim the edge. Hold both the scissors and design loosely.

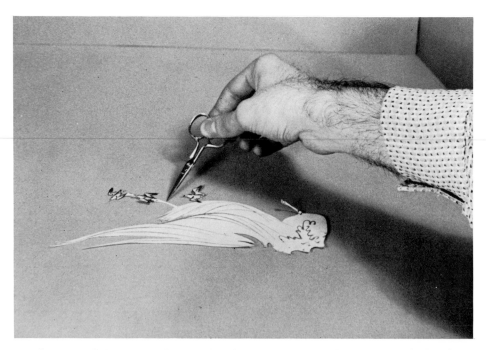

For elements of the design that need to be positioned in relation to the body of the design, as the birds in this scene, or to support thin stems and fine elements, cut bridges as pointed to by the scissors. These bridges are cut away just before gluing. Note also that the edges of the water are feathered with an almost fringelike cutting technique so that the outline is softened somewhat.

ming paper away from the edges. These are not hard and fast rules. Some interior spaces could be cut last, but those decisions come with experience. You should take license with your scissors, eliminating those areas that are not relevant to the design, but this does not mean that cutting should be sloppy. Details should remain crisp and distinguishable. Holding scissors at a slight angle to bevel the edge so that the top surface is longer eliminates the white line that one finds around a cutting and produces a softer result. Cut with the middle of the blade in small slices in an even rhythm rather than with big cuts.

If you have many appendages on the design, stems and the like, that are attached with very slim lines, draw connecting bridges to the mainland of the design and leave these thin strips in place until just before gluing. It keeps dangling stems from breaking off. Another hint: when cutting out very small spaces, prick the space with the point of your scissors from the top to provide an opening for your scissors to find on the underside of the piece. Take your time. Cutting has to be precise.

Gluing

TYPE OF GLUE

There are hundreds of glues on the market and every day finds more. Some are applicable to decoupage, others are not. Generally, a glue should be transparent, non-staining, water-soluble when applied but not water-soluble when dry, and it must stick almost immediately (but not too soon, you need time to manipulate your pieces) and dry soon afterward. The glue must be good for paper, not cause colors to bleed and fade, and stick to wood or whatever surface you are using. An all-purpose glue for wood, metal, acrylic, glass, ceramic, and papier-mâché that meets all these criteria is a polyvinyl acetate (PVA) or even a polyvinyl chloride (PVC) type of glue. These are sold under the trade names of Elmer's glue, Sobo, Duratite (by Dap, Inc.) and so on.

GLUING TECHNIQUES

Before gluing, tack your design into place with Plasti-Tak for a dry run. Plasti-Tak will peel away easily and will not mar the surface. Only if you need to, lightly mark with a pencil where your design should go. When removing design elements, do not forget to peel away the Plasti-Tak. Glue needs to be applied sparingly. Excess glue cakes underneath and causes puckering of the design. There is no overall formula or proportion for glue to water, because different weights or thicknesses and types of papers require different viscosities of glue. If any generalizations can be made, I would recommend three parts of Elmer's glue to one part of water, stirred periodically because the glue settles. Thinner mixtures work better for thinner papers such as rice paper, and thicker mixtures work better for heavy papers such as printing papers (used for original etchings and lithographs). Sometimes, glycerine (purchased in the drugstore) should be added instead of water if you need to retard drying, such as in gluing the inner part of a vase or cylinder that is to become a lamp. Any precise gluing that requires extended manipulation of the design should be slowed down by adding glycerine to the PVA (polyvinyl acetate) glue or mucilage, whichever is your preference. Glycerine is best used with restraint because it acts as a separator for varnish and needs to be cleaned off quite thoroughly.

Remember the above suggestions are generalizations, not absolutes; there are too many exceptions. Start with these suggestions, however, and break the rules as you develop more experience.

To begin, mix your glue in a small container such as a cup or a Pyrex custard dish. Have on hand small sponges, a soft brush, paper toweling, a small roller (optional), a stainless steel or agate burnisher (optional), your glue, water, and glycerine (optional).

Remember that glue should be applied sparingly and no air bubbles should remain under your design. Air bubbles can ruin your work by popping up in an unsightly way later. Your fingers are your best tools. In

Decoupaging a Whole Picture

This coloring book picture, reproduced from a medieval block print by Dover, was colored with the strong colors favored in medieval times, using oil-colored pencils. Then, with a straight-bladed embroidery scissors, excess paper is trimmed away from the print.

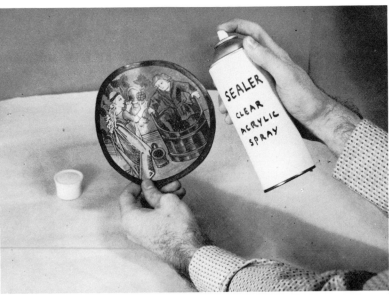

Two to three thin coats of a clear acrylic sealer are sprayed over the picture to preserve and protect the color and surface. When dry, the picture is ready for gluing.

The back of the print also is sprayed. Since the paper is thick enough to be opaque, the print on the back does not bleed through and interfere with the design on the front.

Acrylic sealer is also sprayed on the wooden plate to separate the coating already on the plate from future coatings of varnish. An alcohol-diluted coating of shellac can also be brushed on as a wood sealer. Shellac needs about 24 hours to dry, acrylic less than 10 minutes.

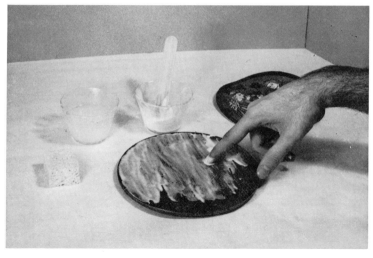

After the sealer has dried, mix your glue (PVA) with water, have sponge and clean water ready, and spread the diluted glue on the plate with your fingers. If the glue beads up in places to reveal the background, you have too much water in your mixture. Add a bit more glue.

When the glue completely covers the plate, immediately place the design on the plate, starting at one end. With a sponge, work the print down until it is attached firmly. For larger areas, *lightly* roll a brayer over the surface to squeeze out some extra glue and air, but do not use too much pressure or there will be no glue left.

Sponge away all excess glue. When dry, your edges as well as the whole piece should be permanently affixed to the plate. If any edges pull away, add more glue and some momentary pressure. Do not move to the next step until the piece is completely glued.

A clear polyurethane (with a slight amber tint) by Sapolin was used for this piece. Varnishes from yesteryear were also amber, hence the "golden" patina of old pieces. Note that the varnish was applied from the center to the edge.

After six coats are applied, wet-sand (#400) the entire piece, but concentrate on the design area, in order to sink the print. Then dust with tack cloth and continue varnishing.

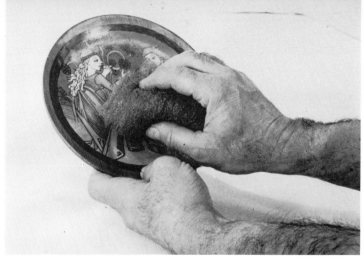

When enough coats have built up to sink or bury the print, wet-sand again and refine your sanding with #000 or #0000 steel wool. Steel wool gets into spots not easily reached with the stiffer sandpaper.

Complete the job by applying wax with a damp flannel cloth.

The completed plate by the author is decorative, but can be used for serving because polyurethane is impervious to almost anything.

most cases, apply glue to the object's surface, rather than to the design, but there are exceptions here, too, particularly when you are working with stiff materials such as foils (apply glue to both surfaces) or on very small elements (apply glue to the element).

Dip your finger into the glue and then spread it thinly over only the immediate area in process. You can also apply glue with a soft watercolor brush made of camel's hair, rabbit hair, sable, or the like. If the glue separates or forms bubbles, add more glue, you have too much water in your mixture. Rinse your fingers in clear water so that your sticky fingers do not stick to the design. You should not have more than a minute altogether before the glue is fixed. Then position your design onto the thin film of glue. You should be able to slide your design around. With a damp sponge, press the design into place, squeezing out all air bubbles and excess glue in the process. Start in the middle and work toward outside edges, repeating the process all around from center outward. If edges pop up, then hold them firmly in place for another moment with your fingers or use the back side of your fingernail to press it in place. Sometimes a spot needs another touch of glue. Apply that with the tip of your brush or a toothpick. Continue to massage your design with your wet fingers until it is flat, free of air bubbles, and is completely adhered to the surface. Follow contours as much as possible, running your fingers along stems, for example, rather than across the stem. Remember to keep your fingers free of glue. Sometimes it is necessary to lightly roll a small printing roller over large surface areas, to press out air and glue. But be careful not to press too heavily and squeeze out all the glue. If an edge still is difficult to glue, put a piece of waxed paper over the design and, with a burnisher or back of a spoon, press the edge onto the surface. After the design has set for a few minutes, clean up around the design with a clean sponge and warm water or cotton swab for fine areas, and allow the glue to dry for at least five hours or overnight. To be certain that the design has completely adhered to your surface, give edges the fingernail test.

To any parts that come loose, apply glue with a toothpick. If you notice any air bubbles, slice into them with a razor and gingerly slip a bit of glue into the slit with a toothpick, press hard with your fingers to adhere the ex-bubble. Continue this process piece after piece until everything is in place. You will not have to do this unless you are grossly careless.

Use tweezers to position small pieces, if necessary. Stubborn glue spots can be removed with a cotton swab that has been dipped in vinegar, but here again, restraint is necessary. Vinegar can cause discoloration of certain paper and dyes because it is an acid.

When gluing large pieces, see about a helper to hold the paper as you press it into place. Begin on one side, top or bottom, apply glue to small areas at a time while someone holds the design away, then press the design into place in the usual manner and continue gluing, pressing small areas at a time.

Try not to overlap designs, it adds too much thickness and then requires too many layers of varnish. Here again there are exceptions, particularly if you do not intend to completely embed the design.

Put trims and fine details on last. Gold embossed braids and ornaments need to be glued tightly and flatly. Let the glue get tacky on both surfaces first, before setting them in place. Rollers are handy for these metallic strips. To turn gold metallic into silver, just use a bit of acetone or nail polish remover over the surface.

When gluing mother-of-pearl, you will note that the pieces curve slightly. Glue the curved side toward the surface and flatten it with your fingers.

After the Gluing Processes

If you want to hand-paint elements, draw lines and borders, or ink your name on the piece, now is the best time, before varnishing. But if you forget, you can still paint over varnish with acrylic and still use ink over varnish as well. Of course, you will have to varnish over your hand-painted elements as well.

Watercolored Decoupage Decoration

Watercolor works quite well on paper that will accept watercolor. Color in background and light colors first; let details and shadows follow. Since watercolor can smear when water-based glues are applied, make certain that the piece is amply protected with acrylic sealer.

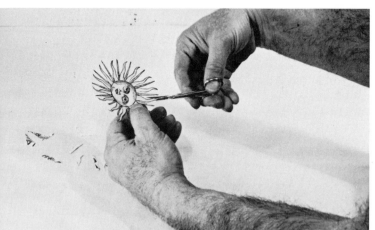

Cut away the background making certain that the black outline that is intrinsic to this block-print design is not destroyed in the process. Also keep corners crisp with definite angles.

The final design by the author was adjusted to fit into the concavity of this rosewood box.

54

Some authorities recommend spraying the glued piece with sealer after the glue has dried thoroughly, but I do not think it necessary, if the design was properly sealed in the first place and all the excess glue is sponged away. Edges that appear white should be touched up with pencil or acrylic paint. No sealing is necessary after this step.

CHANGING YOUR MIND

If something does not work, do not wait until the glue has completely set because PVA glues are not easy to remove. To remove a piece, saturate it with warm water for two or three minutes and then with the help of a knife, starting at one edge, lift it away gently, using more water if necessary. Take your time. If the piece has completely set, forget it.

Varnishing

The Venetians used a glossy and durable oil varnish made of copal or lac suspended in oil and then allowed the varnish to dry in the sun. Europeans of the 18th century imported lacquers from China and Japan which were made from the sap of the *rhus vernicifers* until they could create a varnish that was its equal.

Varnish, as defined by the *Random House Dictionary*, is the overall term that covers transparent coating, including lacquers as well. Today classic varnishes have lost their market to improved and marvelous varnishes made of polymers of various kinds. (See the chart of coatings to clarify and discuss the properties of each.)

For decoupage, varnishes need to be either glossy or mat, crystal clear (slight amber or straw color is tolerable), mar resistant, elastic, heat-proof, and as alcohol-proof as possible.

Generally, glossy varnish is cut by the diluent marked on the label, often by 40 percent, which is usually turpentine or mineral spirits. Mat varnish usually contains wax, pulverized mica, and talc to reduce its luster. Some of the most durable varnishes today are predominantly alkyds, vinyls,

Pre-Colored Cutout for Decoupage

This small wooden box was first sanded and then painted black with acrylic paint. After the paint was completely dry (at least 24 hours), a design which had been cut and sealed with acrylic sealer was adhered to the box with PVA glue. Note that there is no hardware on the box and that masking tape is used to hold the lid in place.

After the print is completely affixed and the glue firm but not too hard, with a sharp knife or razor blade, cut to separate the design at the juncture of lid and box.

Rest the box on a can and coat with varnish starting from the center each time and working the brush outward with an arc-like movement. A clear vinyl varnish was used.

An acrylic mirror is decorated with wrapping paper, colored paper, and embossed metallic stripping. The design is then protected with an acrylic emulsion coating.

Fran Willner's three-dimensional print became the components for this box tailored by the author. Vinyl is used to embed the paperwork.

Art nouveau book illustrations, hand-colored, enhance the drawers of this chest.

This end table utilizes traditional decoupage technique while incorporating the latest in coating technology. Botanical flower illustrations, precisely cut, are glued onto stained mahogany and embedded under 24 layers of phenolic varnish.

This papier-mâché bowl has a design adhered and coated with epoxy. The finish is not too different from a ceramic glaze.

Some primitive animals decorate a purse that has other design elements painted in acrylic and drawn in India ink. By the author.

Maxima Minnie, by the author and her son Lee, is a papier-mâché pop art figure clothed in decoupage and coated with varnish.

A stoneware ceramic bowl decorated with wrapping paper flowers that blend as if they were fired into the glaze when, in fact, the design is decoupage with a sprayed urethane mat finish.

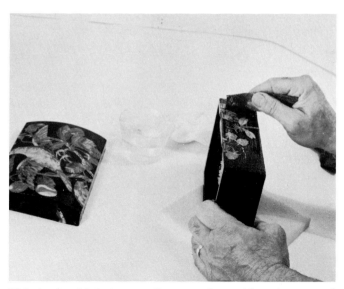

This is the third time sanding was done. After 15 coats of varnish and two sanding operations, the edges of the print could not be felt and the print was buried in the varnish. Then two coats of McCloskey's eggshell varnish were added to impart a mat finish. The box was rubbed with steel wool.

Hardware was attached; and the lining was glued into place to complete the job.

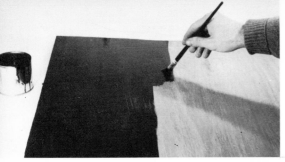

Random Design with Decoupage

A solid mahogany board was painted with a water and alcohol-soluble black translucent dye. The black blended with the reddish brown of the mahogany to create a very dark brown with the grain pattern of the wood still slightly evident.

After the stain completely dried, the table was sealed with WaterLox. Meanwhile, flower prints were precisely cut (it took many, many days) and then arranged and rearranged so that negative and positive spaces related to one another and so that these dissimilar elements created a line of direction for the eye to travel along, as well as a unified overall pattern.

Held in place temporarily with Plasti-Tak, a white putty-like material that does not affect surfaces, each flower was glued into place. Excess glue was then carefully cleaned off.

After five coats of a phenolic called Fabuloy, a very hard covering, the entire table was hand-sanded with #400 wet-or-dry sandpaper. After five more coats of phenolic were applied, a straight-line belt sander was used to gently sand away high spots and to level the coating.

phenolics, and, one of my favorites for furniture, polyurethane. Polyurethane is a very tough material and is difficult to sand, but the resulting surface is impervious to almost everything, including rollerskates.

Many of these varnishes polymerize (harden) when exposed to air. So it is a good idea to buy small cans, or to transfer amounts to small jars that can be filled to the brim and be used for each application. To prevent a skin from forming on the varnish in the can, pour pure distilled turpentine into the surface, just enough to cover the surface, *if that is the diluent*, or mineral spirits, if that is used. It sits on the surface and prevents the air from polymerizing the varnish. Do not try to store varnish for a long time and try to buy fresh varnishes from your paint supplier. If a varnish tends to be amber, you can somewhat minimize its yellowness by adding a *tinge* of cobalt blue oil paint to the can.

Varnishing is a long-range process because decoupage requires many coats, sometimes 20 to 30. Each coat needs 24 hours to dry. Setting up an assembly-line of projects to be done saves some time. Decoupage also requires "elbow grease" because of the number of times pieces need to be sanded. For traditional decoupage results, do not use short cuts, but look into the following chapters for many variations on the theme of decoupage. One innovation is a crystal clear epoxy coating that can save a month of work and can produce results equal to the best of traditional decoupage.

THE VARNISHING PROCESS

The varnishing process is a precise art. Gather your materials—a chiseled oxhair varnish brush (buy the best; it pays), varnish, tack cloth, solvent, a can in which to suspend your brush, and other cans on which to suspend your object. Work in a dust-free, dry room at 70°F. Dust your work with tack cloth.

You can use the same brush for various varnishes as long as the solvent is the same. Do not mix brushes for lacquer, water, and mineral spirits or turpentine. Use separate brushes for each.

Ten more coats of Fabuloy were applied with a nylon stocking pad, enough build-up to sink the prints. Then after a final hand-sanding with #400 wet-or-dry sand-paper, linseed oil and rottenstone were mixed together into a loose paste. The mixture was applied in a cir-cular motion using a padding of flannel. The last scratches were removed and the surface was smooth and flat.

Butcher's wax on a damp cloth was rubbed on, and when dry, the table was buffed to a glossy finish with a damp soft cloth.

A structural aluminum frame was attached.

The final table was mounted on an aluminum base and is ready for use.

Isabel O'Neil recommends loading your brush by dipping it in the jar up to one-third the length of its bristles. Press excess out on the inner side of the jar rather than across the top edge, to keep tiny air bubbles from becoming entrapped in the bristles.

To apply the varnish, start your stroke in the middle of the surface, moving your brush toward the outer edge in a arc-like gesture, traveling with the grain of the wood. The second stroke starts at the same middle point and carries the remaining varnish the same way toward the opposite edge. Continue until you need to recharge your brush with varnish and proceed in the same manner. Do not wipe your brush on a cloth or paper towel because it will pick up lint. Rather, squeeze out bristles with your fingers.

Each successive stroke is brushed in the opposite direction; first with the grain, then across the grain, then with the grain, and so on. Each varnish stroke should be as scant as possible, according to Isabel O'Neil, an expert on furniture finishing. After the first few coats of varnish have been applied with a brush, you could use a pad made of a nylon stocking as an applicator. Very thin coats of varnish are laid this way with almost no air bubbles.

Thicker, more viscous varnishes are apt to entrap more air than thinner varnishes. But the thinner varnishes are slower to build up. Heavy applications of thin varnishes cause excessive running down sides.

Another varnishing technique that works is to thin your varnish with a bit of its diluent and then scrub it in with your brush vigorously, until the bubbles disappear. This thinner application requires more coats.

Mat varnishes always need to be stirred. Use a clean tongue depressor or Popsicle stick. But glossy varnishes do not always require stirring. Check the label on the can. Most applications require 24 hours for drying time. But with urethanes, if you exceed 24 hours until the next application, you have to sand the surface lightly. Again, read the label.

Apply six to ten coats of varnish, depending upon the thickness of your varnish, before attempting to sand. For the first sanding, make a mixture of soap flakes and water, and use #400 wet-or-dry sandpaper. The soap flakes act as an emulsion. You can also dry sand. When the surface is smoother, rinse and dry the object. Wipe the piece with tack cloth and proceed to varnish again. Be very careful not to sand down to your print. Build your coats to at least 15. But after every 5 or 6 coats, do your sanding.

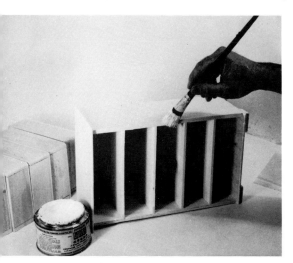

Acrylic Gesso Covering for Raw Wood
This great little chest made in Italy and distributed by Marie Mitchell was made of a hard, rough wood. The grain was not interesting, so the best solution was to coat it with gesso. Two coats of acrylic gesso were applied to all surfaces.

After the second coat, the chest was wet-sanded (#220) to smooth out brushstrokes.

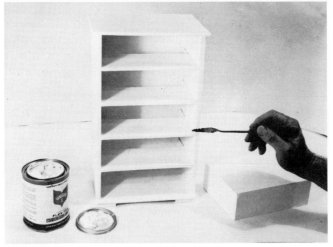

Further imperfections were filled with acrylic modeling paste, using a painting knife.

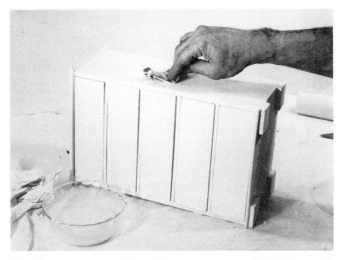

Another two coats of acrylic gesso were added. For each layer, the strokes were applied in crossing directions, at right angles. Then the entire chest was wet-sanded. The drawers were fitted and sanded so that they opened and closed easily to accommodate further layers of paint and varnish.

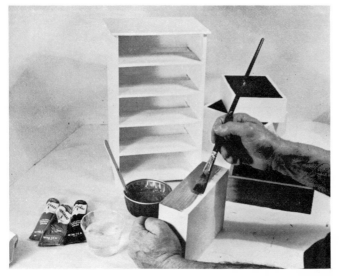

A base coat of translucent light yellow-green acrylic was applied. Then with a stiff bristle brush a second coat was streaked over the first, except on the front of the drawers. These were painted in the same color but without texture. A textured coat on the drawers would have been too distracting because the floral panels were so greatly detailed. The interiors of the drawers were painted a brownish-orange color.

Hand-colored and cut out, the floral elements were sprayed *after* cutting because the sealer rendered that particular coated paper too brittle for cutting fine details. (The book they came from was old.)

After the floral elements were applied with PVA, and the entire chest varnished 20 times with a vinyl varnish, varnishing was completed with two coats of an eggshell varnish to leave a mat finish. Then after sanding and waxing, the chest was ready for hardware. The drawer shape was outlined on paper.

Then the outline was cut out and two diagonals were drawn from corner to corner.

The intersection indicated the center of the drawer. A mark was pierced into the wood with an awl and the fixture was screwed into place.

The 3M Company makes a white rough material called Scotch-Brite that can take the place of steel wool for final sandings. What you are doing in sanding is lowering the coat level over the design, but not around it, to help sink, bury, or embed the design with successive coats of varnish.

The last two or three coats should be a mat varnish. You can achieve a mat surface with #000 or #0000 steel wool, but it is much more difficult than brushing on a few more layers of varnish.

Clean your brush thoroughly with fresh solvent and put it away. If you are working continuously, find a can that has a polyethylene lid, like those used for coffee. Cut a cross in the center of the lid to hold the brush handle and suspend your brush in the solvent to the ferrule. Do not let the brush touch bottom; it will lose its shape. Change the solvent when it begins to yellow. There is usually a gummy residue on the bottom of the can that also has to be cleaned away.

To eliminate faint scratches made by steel wool or sandpaper, mix a light paste of rottenstone or pumice powder with lemon oil or linseed oil, and apply it in a circular motion by hand or on a pad of flannel, felt, or nylon stocking. This produces a superb finish.

Finally, apply a clear wax (turpentine base) such as Butcher's Wax on a dampened piece of flannel. Allow the wax to dry and buff with another clean, damp piece of cotton flannel.

Some specifics: always varnish the inside with a few coats, even if you are going to apply a lining, to prevent warping caused by different contraction and expansion ratios.

Do not put anything on top of your piece when it is dry. It takes at least four weeks for final maturing of surfaces.

Apply two coats of varnish to paper linings, after spraying them with protective sealer and after they are glued into place.

When coating a box, check the underside, edges and sides for drips or build-up. Wipe it way with a sponge dampened with the solvent.

Keep work on a level surface.

You should enjoy the results of your labor, producing a very handsome piece that could last for more than a lifetime.

The final chest by the author, with hand-colored art nouveau designs on the drawers.

DECOUPAGE CLINIC

Malady	Reason	Remedy
Bloom or cloudiness on varnish surface	Might be due to mixture of original product.	Wash with warm water and detergent, dry and wax.
Bubble or lifted piece of design under varnish	Not enough glue under the design.	If the bubble is large enough, with a very sharp and pointed knife, cut around the bubble to remove it dome-shaped; drop a bit of glue on the surface underneath, replace the piece, holding it in place and flatten; wipe away all glue; then remove wax from entire object and revarnish with several coats; and finish as in traditional decoupage.
Chipped varnish	Result of a sharp blow.	Sand surface surrounding chip with #500 grit wet-or-dry sandpaper and then with a very fine steel wool and turpentine to remove wax and mat finish. With a small brush drop one or two drops of varnish in the chip and let it dry. Repeat until the hole is filled, brimming a bit over the surface. Let dry, sand with #400 wet-or-dry sandpaper over the entire piece, then with steel wool (#0000). Apply two thin coats of mat varnish over the entire piece. Sand again and rewax.
Cracking	Caused by shrinkage of the film or undercoat not thoroughly dry.	Let it get bone dry, then continue to varnish; if it is an old piece, sand away wax with #0000 steel wool and apply more coats of varnish until cracks disappear. Sand again and wax.
Dust and brush hairs	Tack cloth not used to clean piece after sanding; brush is old or poor quality and going bald.	Sand down with #400 grit wet-or-dry sandpaper; clean and revarnish.

DECOUPAGE CLINIC (Continued)

Malady	Reason	Remedy
Lumps and bumps	Old varnish left on brush; or hardened lumps in the can of varnish.	Try to scrape it away. Let it dry thoroughly, then sand with #400 grit wet-or-dry sandpaper and apply more coats of varnish, until lumps disappear; sand again and wax.
Marks and dents, lines and patterns of different shapes	Made by placing things on the varnished piece before it thoroughly dried.	Sand and revarnish.
Objects or edges showing through varnish	Sanded too much at corners and edges; skimped on varnish.	Touch up print with paint if needed; touch up the wood sparsely; apply protective sealer; let dry and fill as you would for chipped varnish.
Streaks	Thick and thin areas in the surface underneath the varnish.	No remedy, unless you are willing to remove the varnish and smooth down the areas and then revarnish.
Uneven buildup	Piece was not level when drying and drained to one side.	Sand with #400 wet-or-dry sandpaper; dust; revarnish; sand again and wax.
Varnish runs	Drainage of too much varnish, excess was not picked up when applied.	Slice them off with a razor or knife; then let surfaces dry and continue varnishing.
Warping of the object	Varnishing only on one side builds up tensions and contraction of varnish sets in.	Dampen (if wood) the unvarnished side, place in a plastic bag and seal the bag; put weights on the curved part that needs adjusting, for several days, until it straightens out; then remove from bag and let it dry out with weights on it; varnish heretofore unvarnished part with three coats. Use cabinet clamps for large pieces.
Wrinkles	Perhaps too much varnish applied before the undercoat had a chance to dry.	Do not sand it; just let it dry thoroughly and when dry continue varnishing. Wrinkles will disappear under enough coats of varnish.

BASIC MATERIALS FOR DECOUPAGE

Objects to be decoupaged
Prints and other kinds of design elements
Colored oil pencils or watercolors
Glue
Containers for glue and water
Soft brush for gluing
Sponge, cut into small squares
Water for glue mixture and for cleaning off glue
Plasti-Tak or other stainless, temporary putty for holding design in place
Tack cloth for dusting away specks
Brayer
Ruler and tape measure
Scissors, small, curved and straight blades
X-acto knife or razor blade for cutting design at juncture or lids and miscellaneous jobs
Acrylic paint and stains for coloring objects
Brushes for acrylic paint
Varnishes
Brushes for varnishing
Container for solvent to clean brushes
Solvent, specific to the varnish, usually turpentine, mineral spirits, or lacquer thinner (acetone)
Sealer for the prints (acrylic spray or diluted shellac)
Sealer for woods
#220, #400 wet-or-dry sandpaper
#100, #200 garnet paper
#000, #0000 steel wool
Wax (turpentine base) for polishing

List of Materials
For Advanced Decoupage
Techniques

Acrylic gesso for covering raw wood

Acrylic modeling paste for filling dents and cracks
Wood vinyl filler for filling cracks
Tweezers
Palette knife for applying modeling paste or wood filler
Metallic embossed papers, vinyls, Mylars for trimmings
Fancy papers, leathers, fabrics for coverings, linings, and designs
Modeling tools for relief pieces
Agate or stainless steel burnisher for pressing edges into base
French clay or RTV silicone sealer for relief pieces
Cardboard for base of linings
Rubber cement for attaching linings
Gold leaf
Sodium sulfate for discoloring gold leaf
Dried leaves
Mother-of-pearl
Denatured alcohol for cleaning pieces
Urethane spray
Vinegar
Glossy acrylic spray
Shellac
Rust preventative paint
Pencil sharpener
Waxed paper
Glycerine for extending wet-time of glue
Cotton swabs, toothpicks, and tongue depressors
Rottenstone or pumice
Linseed oil or lemon oil
Straight line or reciprocating sanders (electric)
Findings: hinges, screws, handles, and knobs for objects
Awl
Screwdriver

VARNISH FINISHES

Finishes, Brand Name	Main Component	Soluble in	Compatible with *	Characteristics	Drying Time	Mode of Application
Deft	Lacquer base, nitrocellulose and alkyds	Lacquer thinner	Lacquer, vinyl wood, metal; can be used over other finishes but test first; not good over oil-based paints, glazes, and varnishes. Attacks many dyes. Needs undercoatings.	Clear, bubble-free, hard, water and alcohol resistant, semi-gloss.	30 minutes to touch; 2 hours to next application.	Apply with full wet strokes.
Fabuloy	Phenolic	Turpentine, mineral spirits, or Fabuloy Reducer.	Used as a floor finish, excellent for wood, Masonite, on porous surfaces use a base coat.	Very hard, resistant to water; durable coating, used for floors; light, transparent amber.	4 hours between coats.	Do not mix or stir; apply in thin coats, room temperature. In partly filled container a skim forms on top unless 1 ounce pure turpentine is poured into container before sealing.
Flair Finish O-P Craft	Terpolymers (a mixture of three kinds of plastics)	Water	Over wood, cardboard, paper, metal, stone. Compatible with most art materials.	Clear, quick build-up; tends to be bubbly. Requires a turpentine-based varnish for a final hard finish.	45 minutes between coats.	Bristle brush or sponge applicator; flow on coats barely touching surface; do not brush back and forth; do not shake or stir; sand after every 3 coats to break air bubbles only.

Product	Composition	Thinner	Use over surfaces	Characteristics	Drying time / coats	Mixing and application
Flourish Decoupage Finish	Acrylic and another unnamed polymer	Water	Wood, metal, plastics such as acrylic and vinyl. Compatible with most art materials.	Milky at first; easy build-up; not an exceptionally hard finish.	1 hour between coats; 5 hours before sanding; after 4th coat dries overnight; 15 maximum number of coats.	Do not shake or stir; brush with slow flowing stroke barely touching surface; do not brush back and forth; sand after every 3 coats to break air bubbles only.
Fuller O'Brien Pen-Chrome Wood Finishes	Alkyd, phenolic	Mineral spirits or turpentine	Over most oil and wax-free surfaces.	Clear, light amber, a durable finish, builds up slowly.	24 hours between coats	Stir thoroughly but do not shake; soft bristle brush or spray.
Hallmark Art Podge	Same as Mod Podge	Water	Same as Mod Podge	Same as Mod Podge	Same as Mod Podge	No mixing necessary.
Hallmark Decoupage	Not given. Probably a lacquer base	Water	Lacquer, water-soluble bases, clear wood, Masonite.	Very flammable, highly volatile needs a great deal of ventilation. Quantity of solids to solvent low; crystal clear, brushes well, hard finish.	1 hour between coats; 6 hours before sanding.	Few brush strokes as possible; 7 coats sinks print. Do not mix or stir.
McCloskeys Heirloom Eggshell Finish	Alkyd, silicates	Turpentine or mineral spirits	Over most other finishes except wax.	Clear, satin finish, resistant to water and alcohol; excellent as a top coat; also is a sealer as well as a finishing coat.	As a top coat use 2 or 3 coats; dries in about 4 hours.	Stir thoroughly, apply with brush, lambs-wool applicator, or nylon stocking.
McCloskeys Heirloom Vinyl Varnish	Vinyl	Same as above	Same as above	Same as above except a hard, glossy finish.	Allow 24 hours to dry.	Do not shake or stir; brush back and forth as directed; apply 10 coats before sanding.

Finishes, Brand Name	Main Component	Soluble in	Compatible with *	Characteristics	Drying Time	Mode of Application
Mod Podge	Acrylic, vinyl, latex	Water	Acrylic, vinyl, uncoated materials such as paper, wood fabric, cardboard, Masonite, plaster, glass, wax.	Easy to apply; a "fun" finish requires coating of turpentine-based varnish as final finish to protect surface; builds quickly without excess of bubbles; milky color dries clear.	20 minutes between coats; needs to dry until clear; urethane spray coat excellent top coating.	Brushing, no mixing necessary.
Miracle Epoxy crystal clear	2-part epoxy system	Acetone	With most materials except wax.	Clear, exceptionally hard, adhesive and coating; particularly good over difficult and non-absorbent surfaces such as metals and glass.	2 hours between coats; 24 hours before handling.	Mix two parts A & B in equal quantities, apply with painting knife or tongue depressor.
Patricia Nimocks Decoupage	Vinyl	Turpentine or mineral spirits	Wood, metal, glass, acrylic.	Crystal clear, transparent, hard, non-yellowing; easy to apply.	6 hours between coats.	Do not shake or stir; brush back and forward in thin coats; apply 10 coats before sanding.
Polyester Resins water-white laminating types	2-part polyester system	Acetone	Compatible with many finishes, but testing first is urgent; turns papers transparent.	Water-white, glossy, needs to be protected from air when curing, or coated with a highly catalyzed coat to eliminate tacky surface.	30 minutes to 1 hour.	According to manufacturer, polyester and catalyst needs to be mixed thoroughly; limited life in can; for thin coatings, increase amount of catalyst; may be brushed on.
Polyurethane Spray (N.Y. Bronze Powder Co.)	Polyurethane	Turpentine or mineral spirits	New wood, Masonite, over Mod Podge, ceramic, any many other materials.	Clear, very, very hard, long-wearing.	6 to 12 hours between coats.	Spray 12-14 inches away, short, dusting strokes, thin coats, apply at room temperature; shake.

Product	Composition	Solvent	Use Over	Characteristics	Drying Time	Application
Royale Coat Decoupage Finish	Alkyd, silica, cellulose nitrate	Turpentine or mineral spirits	Wood, metal, glass, acrylic; use sealer if applied over oil-based paints or stains.	Crystal clear, transparent, hard finish.	1 hour between coats; 12 to 24 hours before sanding.	Stir thoroughly, but do not shake; brush in one direction with slow flowing motion; refill brush for each stroke; change direction of stroke for each coat.
Sapolin Polyurethane Clear coating satin finish	Polyurethane	Turpentine or mineral spirits	Directly on raw wood, other varnishes, test first.	Begins as a clear, light, amber color, with exposure to air, becomes shellac-like in color and consistency; very hard, durable.	24 hours between coats.	No mixing; brush for interior and exterior.
Vanguard or Liquitex polymer medium	Acrylic emulsion	Water	Over any water-soluble finish; acrylic, paper, gesso, wood.	A milky liquid that dries into a water-clear, hard finish; can be used both as an adhesive and varnish.	1 hour between coats.	Shake before using with brush, sponge, fingers.
Varathane Satin by Flecto	Urethane, stearic acids, etc.	Turpentine or mineral spirits	Over anything but lacquer, shellac, stains containing stearate; good over oil-based paints.	Light amber, extremely hard; interior, exterior use; resists chipping; protects metal from corrosion.	Dust free 30 minutes; drying time 3 hours, recoat 6 hours.	Apply each coat within 24 hours otherwise need to sand first; brush one, each coat 90° change in direction.
WaterLox	Not given	Turpentine or mineral spirits	Varnishes, shellac, lacquer, phenolic; use over wood, concrete, slate, brick, leather, cork, plasterboard metal.	Acts as a sealer and finish; builds up after second coat; transparent; should be put into smaller container as used; resistant to water and alcohol.	24 hours between coats.	Do not shake or mix; brush or apply with lambs wool or nylon stocking.

* If there is any doubt about your material or finish, test your varnish on a sample piece and wait at least one week before making any judgments.

Hiram Manning, one of the original popularizers of decoupage and a master of this art, created the design of this table. Courtesy: Hiram Manning and the Hearthside Press.

Fashion prints have been very popular for traditional decoupage design. This stationery box, colored in burnt orange, was created by Gini Merrill.

Fran Cohen, who studied with Hiram Manning, designed these boxes.

Note how well the design carries through from the top down to the front of this box by Marion Arnao, a student of June Meier's at the Cricket Cage in New Jersey.

This beautifully organized design is by Sylvia Simon.

Dee Davis and Dee Frenkel created this classical design with hand-colored details.

George Ruther designed this container for napkin rings. Every part of it demonstrates meticulous attention to detail in cutting, coloring, and varnishing.

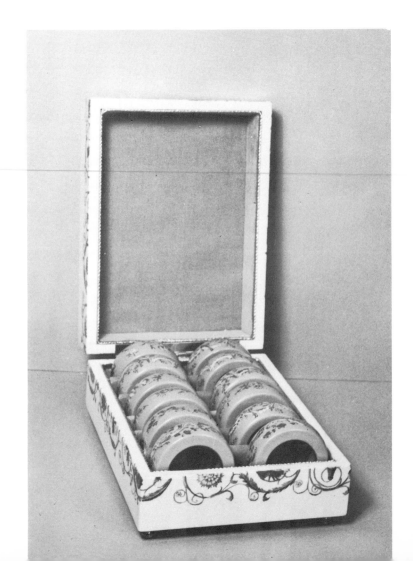

This box was inlaid with specks of mother-of-pearl to dramatize the waterfall. It glistens with its iridescence. Design by Marion Arnao.

Crisp and attractive with a superb finish using Deft, a lacquer-based varnish. Created by Gini Merrill.

Gini Merrill uses birds again as her theme. Note that the line details and grass were hand-painted.

Lee Walker made these two clocks. Note the superb cutting of the fine lines in each of these pieces.

June Meier made this clock using a traditional 18th-century theme.

This five-drawer chest is used for small serving pieces or for jewelry. Gesso was applied over rough wood and sanded smooth, then antiqued with chartreuse. Prints are hand-colored in soft greens. The cherubs on the sides and top are in relief. By Ann Standish.

A chinoiserie design decorates the tissue box and children's book figures top the middle box. All by Gini Merrill.

Here fashion prints adorn a boudoir wastebasket and the egg, which was also a popular 18th-century shape. Both by Gini Merrill.

Hand-colored figures finely cut in the spirit of the chinoiserie designs of the 18th century by Fran Cohen.

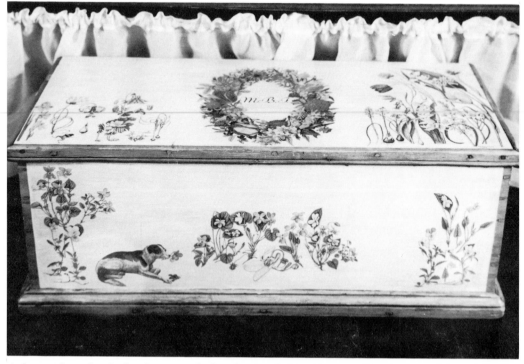

A hope chest by Lydia Irwin with hand-colored floral elements and hand-drawn initials in the wreath.

A firescreen by Gini Merrill. Large units were cut into sections to facilitate handling in cutting and gluing.

Another firescreen, this one by Lydia Irwin who works with Gini Merrill.

A headboard by Lydia Irwin using her favorite floral and animal motifs.

Fran Cohen's 18th-century footstool with an ivory background adorned with painted gold trim and moss green velvet upholstery.

Gini Merrill's boudoir table with fashion prints and hand-painted details.

Another Lydia Irwin hope chest. A kind of playfulness shows up in her treatment of floral-animal subjects.

4

covering
and lining boxes

Boxes and chests that have been decoupaged look precious. Instinctively, one wants to see more and look inside. A lined box projects a more professional, finished appearance. The lining transports the design from the interesting to the magnificent.

Of course, use dictates aspects of lining. A train-case should be lined in a washable material such as padded vinyl, certainly not felt or velvet. But a jewelry box should have a soft-faced lining such as velvet, felt, moiré, or silk. Oriental tea papers make beautiful linings for drawers, boxes, and other general storage pieces.

Lining is a distinctive part of your creation and although it does not have to repeat the materials used on the outside (although it can in the box lid), it should relate in some way with the purposes, style, and colors of the exterior. A fine silk brocade belongs with

a chinoiserie design, whereas burlap can harmonize with a hex design or the like. A bright yellow interior may provide an effective contrast for a black box, but not if there is no suggestion of yellow on the exterior of your design. Although one cannot rule out the use of bright yellow in this case, certainly picking up one of the exterior colors would be more harmonious and the total effect then would be an integrated one.

There are no hard and fast rules about linings except that you should select elegant materials that have interesting textures and patterns. One usually cannot see the interior and exterior of a box at the same time, so there is little danger of two designs fighting for attention. If the lining used is very simple and nondescript, then why not just paint the interior? Certainly paint can be attractive as well.

Some lining and covering materials are fabrics, such as silk brocades, moiré, velvets; felts, leathers, and suedes, flannel, burlap; papers such as wallpapers, posters, tea papers, marbled and tie-dye and block printed paper, and other papers with an overall and repeat design; plastic fabrics such as vinyl; and directly applied materials such as paint, gold leaf, and decoupaged pictures and elements.

Covering a box should be accomplished at the same time as decoupaging, but linings should be applied last, even after hardware is in place, if you wish. The one exception is if you are decoupaging the interior, too.

While coverings should be added directly to the object, linings can be attached directly or better still, on cardboard first and then to the interior of the box.

If your box has a wooden liner, just remove the liner and sand it so that corners will accommodate the fabric thickness that you are going to add. If your box does not have wooden liners, then measurements should be taken of all sides, top, and bottom, and liners can be cut from shirt cardboard or cardboard mat board.

Before beginning, practice with cheap materials or papers and consider your practice piece, if successful, a pattern for the final material.

Specific step-by-step directions follow in photographs and captions. Since there is no one way of lining a box, your specific piece may require departures from these suggestions.

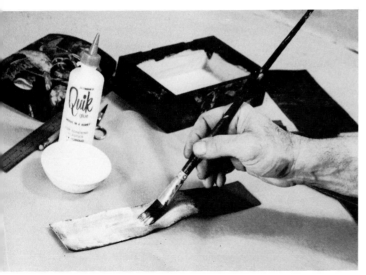

Applying Fabric Directly

This is the simplest technique. Take measurements of your interior spaces— sides and bottom and sides and top in the lid. Translate this to paper to make a pattern. Cut your pattern from paper and then attach it to your fabric; outline your pattern on the fabric, and then cut the lining to size, each piece separately. If your material is thick, you will have to make a slight adjustment for corners. Another approach is to use a continuous strip for all around the sides, or for two sides and the bottom, but be certain that corners fit squarely. Do not try this with fabrics that do not crease well.

All heavy crushed-velvet pieces for the lining are cut to size and have been checked in the box for fitting. Brush a flexible rubber-based or vinyl-based glue on the fabric. Slomons Quik glue was used because it has enough flexibility to permit stretching.

Place sides on first. Smooth out air bubbles.

Next, fit the bottom into place; then the pieces for the lid.

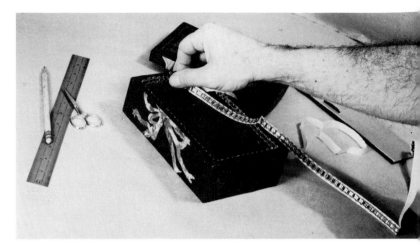

Finish with trim, if you like. This gold vinyl material is self-sticking. Self-sticking lining materials are also available.

Hinges in place, the box sports a moss green crushed-velvet lining.

Flowers are glued to the interior surface and backed with gesso in this glass lamp by John Campbell and Lewis Morrow.

A Josef Albers-type of design in cut paper as a clock face sets the pace.

This black enamel tin for securities was decorated with textured Japanese paper, cut into an exploded design, and coated with urethane.

This "bookcase" by the author is a *trompe l'oeil,* an eye-fooling decoupage illusion.

An apple-shaped rosewood bowl, small enough to fit into the palm of your hand, is topped with a medieval hand-colored sun.

One version of a suede-covered wooden purse that has two alternatives in sliding panels. This panel is of gold leaf with a chemically designed mock-tortoise background and a multiple repoussé star. The stars are adhered and extended into the third dimension with RTV silicone.

This acrylic quadradecahedron was decorated on five sides with Japanese veil paper in a mesh pattern, handcolored with watercolor, and sprayed with an adhesive-coating of acrylic. The design echoes in fascinating images within the polygon.

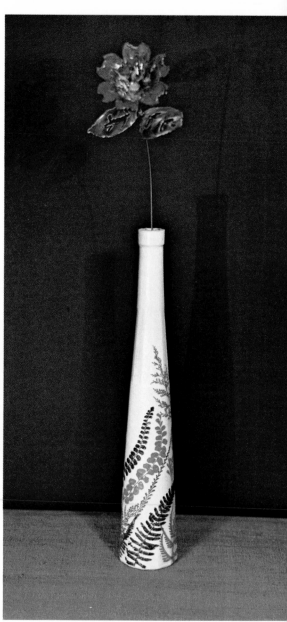

Oshibana (Japanese leaves and collage) is the technique used here in an embedded design on a gesso-covered glass bottle.

Feathered Fury by Carl Federer is done by a fragmentation decoupage process.

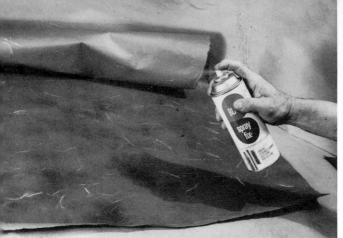

Applying Lining to Cardboard

Japanese paper with a floating silk texture is porous. Spraying the paper on both sides (two coats) is essential. It plugs up the porosity to keep the adhesive from seeping through and the color from bleeding.

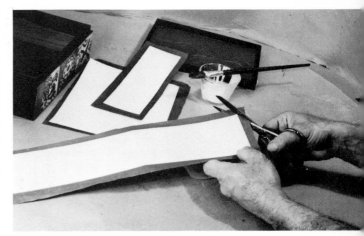

Measure your cardboard pieces to fit the sides, bottom, and top of the box. Cut them, making allowance for the thickness of the material to be wrapped around these pieces. Glue (with rubber cement or other glue) the cardboard to the lining, allowing at least one-half inch extra material around all sides. Take a diagonal slice, cutting an equilateral triangle from each corner, so that when the lining is folded around the cardboard, the corners will meet and not overlap.

Fold down the edges and glue them onto the cardboard base.

Using undiluted PVA here, the sides are fastened into place and then the bottom is added. Note that this lid does not have sides because it fits snugly against a wooden liner that projects above the box and holds the lid in place without hinges.

This box is oval; therefore, the sides are continuous. Note that to curve the fabric around the ovals of the base and lid, notches had to be cut into the fabric. Then when the fabric was turned down, these pieces did not overlap.

Covering a Box with Wallpaper and Embossed Metallic Foil

This wooden tissue box was sanded and then painted with two coats of acrylic paint (by Royal Coat) in dark walnut. Since sides were to be covered, only corners and edges were painted, in addition to the top.

The interior was painted with two coats of white acrylic paint (Vanguard).

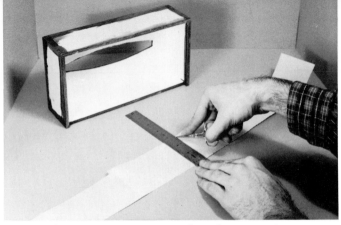

A pattern was measured and cut to fit around the sides. Then metallic wallpaper was cut around the pattern. A scissors was used to score the corners by scratching a line with a scissors point so that the heavy wallpaper would crease easily.

A mixture of PVA and water was spread, one side at a time, directly on the wood.

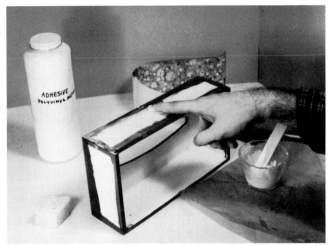

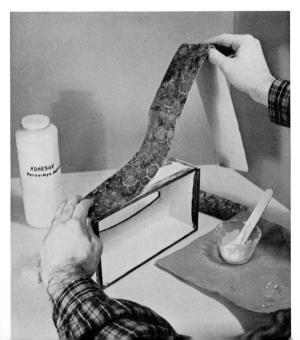

Then the wallpaper was placed on the glued section, starting at one end, pressing and working out bubbles with fingers until the entire piece was attached.

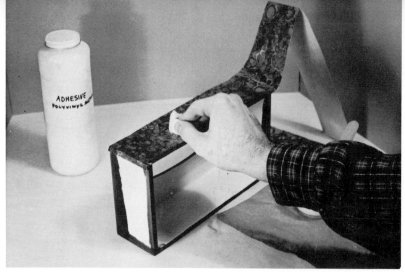

A sponge also is used to press the wallpaper in place and to wipe away excess glue.

After the wallpaper is fully attached, a brayer is rolled lightly to spread the glue and press out whatever bubbles remain.

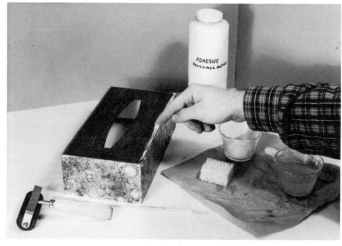

Glue is being placed on the edge of the box and also on the piece of embossed foil stripping that will be used as decoration.

The foil strip is folded to go around the corner and is pressed into place by hand.

The brayer is a mechanical means to affix the stripping.

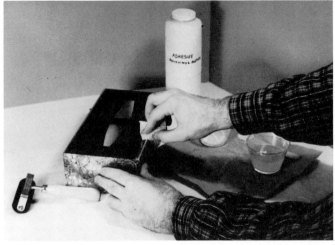

Excess glue is wiped away with a clean sponge and water.

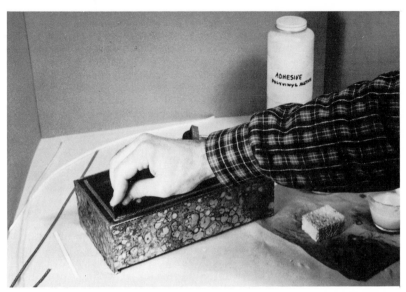

Corners are mitred by overlapping the pieces at right angles and then with a sharp razor slicing a diagonal from outer corner to inner corner. Then the pieces that are cut off are removed and both ends fit perfectly.

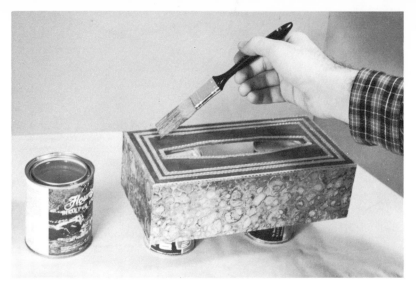

After the foil strips are attached, cleaned of glue, and completely dry, the entire box is covered with a "fun" finish called Flourish. Flourish needs to be flowed onto the box to avoid air bubbles. New coats can be applied every few hours, so that the coating time is greatly reduced. After every six coats have been applied, the piece is wet-sanded (#400) to erase the many bubbles that form in this material. More coats are applied to the top but not the sides, until the desired build-up is achieved. Foil strips are a thick material and it takes at least 20 coats to sink them.

In the final analysis, the finish is a good one and the tissue box is quite handsome.

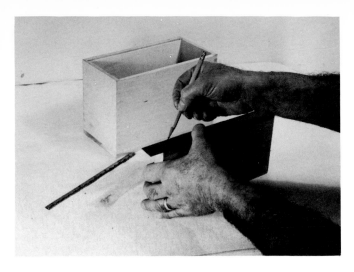

Covering a Box with Leather (Suede)

The wooden box is measured for a piano hinge.

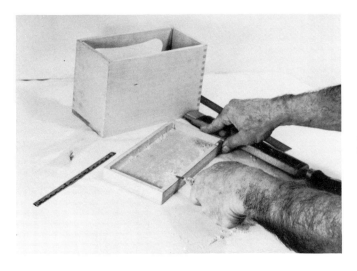

A sliver is cut away, enough to accommodate the thickness of the hinge.

The area is evened and finished off with Surform (Stanley).

A paper pattern is made of the box. It is taped to the leather and then, with an X-acto knife, the piece is cut out.

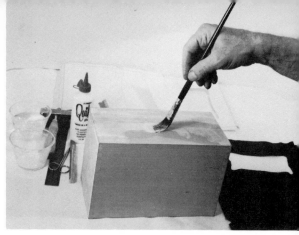

Rubber cement or a PVA-based glue is brushed onto the wooden box, just on one side at a time.

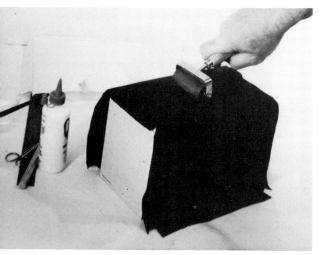

The suede is fitted onto that portion of the box-purse which is the base, and a brayer is rolled over the surface to even out the glue and press out air bubbles.

When that piece has been completely glued to the sides, edges are glued, stretching the leather tightly around the corners. To fit the suede around the curves of this front panel, slits have to be made in the curved areas. After this has been glued into place, the side pieces are attached. To make the leather fit snugly at the ends, without the thickness of the leather showing around the sides and front, the leather edges are thinned down with a knife, shaving off as much as possible, one-half inch in from the edge, so that all that is left of the edge is a paper-thin thickness. When glued, the edge "melts" into the other parts showing hardly any demarcation of a seam.

Lining a Box with a Continuous Lining

Cardboard pieces are cut to measure—bottom, top, and sides, accommodating for the thickness of this silk brocade lining material. The cardboard is then glued into place on the fabric allowing about a half inch of fabric to project all around and leaving a gap of one-eighth inch between pieces to permit the cardboard just to match at the corners and not to overlap when folded into a box shape. Then the edges are turned back and glued as in the other procedures, and the entire back of the lining is brushed or sprayed with rubber cement, as is the box. In a few moments, the lining is pressed into place.

Three boxes by Gini Merrill, beautifully lined. The one on the left is lined with python-printed vinyl and the other two with Scalamandre silk brocades.

This box by Marion Arnao has a velvet lining. Two sides are continuous with the bottom following the interior curve of the box.

Fran Willner covered this old chest with fine block-printed paper outside and inside of the drawers as well.

The outside of this antique chest was covered as well with the same paper. Then the entire piece was varnished several times.

5

oriental and contemporary themes with variations

After the traditional decoupage techniques have been mastered, license can be taken with design, materials, and processes to create individual and unusual works of art. If a method is so confining that it hamstrings an expression or an idea, then it has to be modified. That is the way to keep a concept viable, growing, changing, and open-ended.

Most of the processes described in this chapter are traditional, with design being the point of departure. Some projects depict an approach with an Oriental influence, not of the chinoiserie genre, but in an "Eastern," stylized interpretation. Some other variations use "fun" finishes and unusual backgrounds such as corrugated cardboard and gold leaf.

Subsequent chapters make further adjustments in process, but let us look at some design possibilities first.

A good way to begin is to work with whole pictures. Very little cutting is necessary when you try your hand at developing a

prowess with varnish. Cutting does require precision and time. Therefore, if you want to be certain about the effectiveness of technique or material, use a whole picture.

One excellent way to break away from formal design formats is to try Oriental themes. Although highly traditional, there is a quality to Oriental art that gets to the essence of an idea in form, color, and gesture with the use of fascinating textures in papers and informal balance in design. Note the way the object is juxtaposed against space.

Contemporary themes can jump off from this point. In fact, Oriental design has had a strong influence in contemporary art. This need not be the case. Although most of the examples in this chapter are contemporary in nature, they are not, for the most part, modern. Their subject matter has a timeless quality, with a "now" look using recognizable symbols.

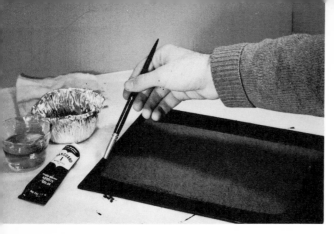

Use of a Whole Picture

In preparation for making place mats, one dozen pieces of Masonite were cut to size, edges were sanded, and with a thin coating of acrylic paint that was diluted somewhat with water, the outside border was painted black.

When the acrylic was dry, the Masonite was sprayed on both sides with a clear acrylic sealer.

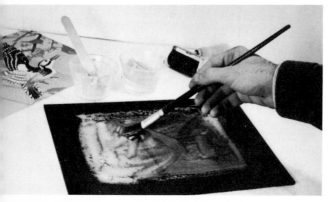

When the sealer dried thoroughly, the entire piece was brushed with PVA. Note that the beading indicates that too much water was used in the glue mixture and that more glue was needed.

The prints also were sprayed with sealer. Starting from the center, the print was smoothed down toward each end with a sponge.

When the entire print was adhered, excess glue was washed away with a sponge and water.

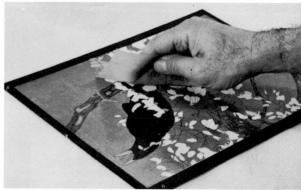

Hallmark decoupage finish was applied to the surface every hour and a half until 10 coats were built up. Then the entire piece was sanded with #400 grit wet-or-dry sandpaper and then with #600 Mylar-backed wet-or-dry (Flexi-grit) sandpaper.

Five of a dozen place mats with very colorful Japanese bird prints by Rakusan Tsuihiya (Foster Art Print Book).

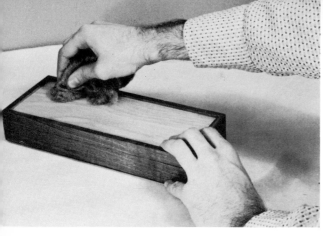

Hand Print on Handmade Japanese Paper

A long box with sides of solid walnut and a recessed top of pine was prepared for decoupage by sanding with #400 grit wet-or-dry sandpaper and then refining this with #000 steel wool.

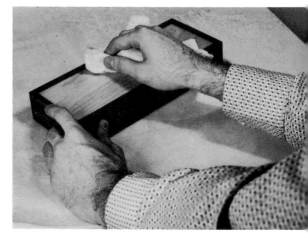

Dust was removed with a tack cloth.

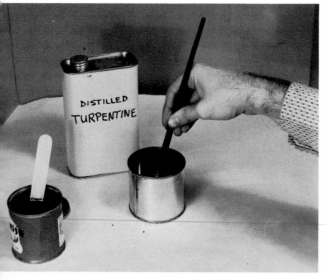

A black copal varnish (the old-fashioned variety) was thinned somewhat with turpentine . . .

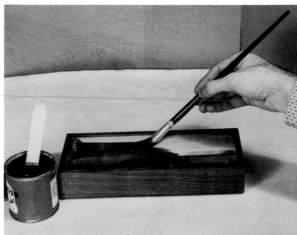

and was brushed onto the pine top of the box, applying three coats until it was fully opaque.

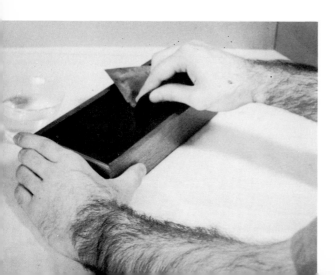

When dry, the surface was sanded smooth with #400 sandpaper and dusted with tack cloth.

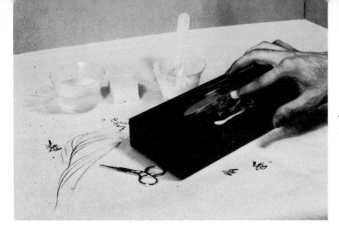

Then PVA glue was spread by finger to the area that was to accept the design.

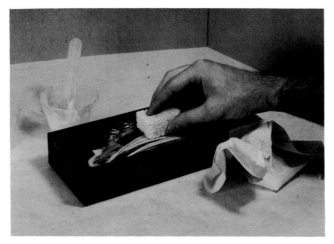

An original Japanese print on rice paper was cut out, sprayed with sealer, and then added to the surface, with informal balance carried out reproducing the position of these elements as they appeared on the print.

Polyurethane was brushed onto the surface, starting from the center and working out toward the edges. Note that not enough sealer was sprayed on the print, and it became saturated with urethane (but this finally dried almost to the original color).

After 15 coats and intermittent sanding of #400 and #500 wet-or-dry sandpaper (using it wet), the piece was ready for refinement to an even smoother finish.

A rottenstone and linseed oil mixture was scoured on the surface via a piece of flannel.

After the linseed oil mixture was wiped away, a mat wax was applied with a damp piece of flannel onto the surface and the piece was buffed.

Result: a very precious box.

Gold Leafing

A laminated wooden plate was prepared for gold leafing by sanding the surface and then by cleaning away fingerprints with denatured alcohol.

Glue can be used as an adhesive for the gold leaf, but I used varnish instead. A vinyl varnish is being brushed onto the surface with the grain of the wood.

Starting from the center section at one end, a leaf of gold is laid in place; then the next leaf and the next until the entire piece is covered.

With a light brushing, the leaf is pressed into place.

Then the gold-leaf backing is peeled away. Take care to be certain that the gold leaf has been adhered completely, otherwise it will pull away later in varnishing.

Flowers are cut and design-adjusted to the plate and glued. Then the same vinyl varnish used to adhere the gold leaf is employed to coat the plate. The design is sunk in the traditional way and the whole piece is sanded and waxed, producing this result.

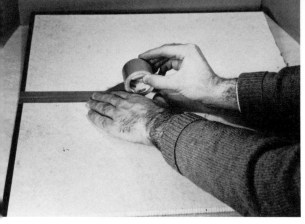

A Cardboard Screen with a "Fun" Finish

A Dritz (TRaum #8098) cutting board of corrugated paper was cut in half because I wanted a shorter screen. Plastic tape was used to reinforce the seams and edges.

Then Mod Podge (a vinyl "fun" finish) was coated over the entire piece, front and back, to seal the surfaces.

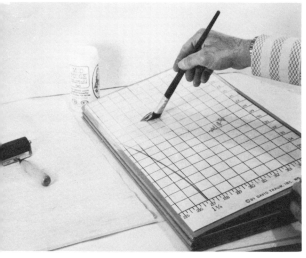

Mod Podge was also used as an adhesive for the natural grass wallpaper for the back.

The wallpaper was applied starting at the top and working out air bubbles by hand, until the entire piece was attached.

Then a brayer was used to eliminate the rest of the bubbles and to squeeze out excess glue.

The same procedure was repeated for the other side. Mod Podge was used again as the adhesive.

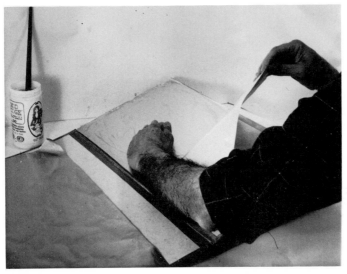

A metallic-topped paper was selected for the background; it was cut to size and applied the same way as the wallpaper.

Excess Mod Podge was sponged away with water. Air bubbles were pressed out.

Flowers that were cut from another Foster book on Oriental flowers were used. They are being glued into place, also with Mod Podge.

Excess is sponged away with water. Note that the design is positioned the same way on the background as a Japanese traditional print would be on paper.

Another "fun" finish is used to embed the print (O. P. Craft Flair) with five coats.

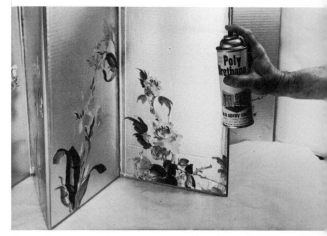

For a harder surface, two coats of polyurethane are sprayed on.

The final screen lights up the area. It cannot be considered a fine art piece, because an inexpensive backing and a fun finish were used, but rather one that is adequate for display purposes. The question that needs to be asked is: Did it pay to spend so much time cutting out those flowers for a temporary effect?

Informal Balance, Japanese Style

These fish came from a Japanese book of original prints. They were sprayed with acrylic sealer and adhered to this wooden tray with PVA in an informally balanced design (See Chapter 2). Then after coating the piece with 15 coats of vinyl varnish, the last three coats of eggshell varnish for a mat effect were applied with a padding of nylon stocking.

This process results in a marvelous finish and a very handsome tray.

This small handcarved wooden dish is decorated with elements from an Oriental print. The finish is vinyl and the piece was designed and executed by the author.

This handsome solid walnut cocktail table (15″ x 51″ x 22″) is decorated with "Fantasy Flower" prints arranged in an Oriental style, balancing elements informally. The prints were colored with a 20-pencil palette using strong pastels. The artist is Marie Mitchell.

Inside and outside are coordinated in this handsome walnut silver chest which also has an Oriental quality. The design is in shades of orange, terra-cotta, and turquoise and the interior is lined in turquoise velvet. By the master decoupeur, Marie Mitchell.

This gold-leaf tray inspired by an Oriental design was created by Dee Davis and Dee Frenkel.

Use of an Original Embossed Print

The original print for this redwood box was by Fran Willner. It was a large print of embossed rectangular units in black and white with a strip of orange. These were cut and reassembled to fit the box. The print was printed on a thick paper that was not thinned. Since redwood sometimes bleeds through, thick paper may provide some protection.

Meanwhile, the box was stained with water-alcohol soluble black stain (Solar-Lux by Factual Finish) and sealed with WaterLox, a transparent penetrating sealer. After the print was sealed and glued into place, ten coats of vinyl varnish and two coats of egg-shell finish were applied. The eggshell varnish was applied with a nylon stocking. There was not enough varnish applied to destroy the embossed quality of the print, but enough to provide a protec-tive finish. Because the print was embossed, #ooo steel wool was used to sand the uneven surfaces.

After a sanding application of rottenstone and linseed oil, and then a waxing, the box was lined and ready for use.

Superimposing Design Elements

For a spot of humor, a wooden plaque was decorated using yesteryear (but made today) Hallmark gift wrap paper as a background, an embossed girl dressed in the clothing of the same period as the background (printed in Germany), and Mylar rickrack. The background was applied to the plaque which was stained with dark walnut acrylic, and the embossed girl figure was adhered next.

Rickrack was attached all around to frame the edge and to add another ludicrous note to the whole piece. Everything was varnished with a latex-based varnish.

The result is a giggle.

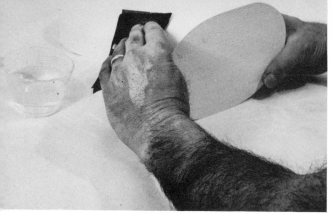

Cutouts with Painted and Drawn Background

This oval wooden box, made by the Morris Manufacturing Company, was sanded smooth.

The entire piece was painted with two coats of a warm yellow-ivory acrylic paint.

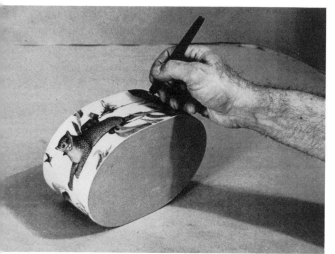

Elements from a print, some grass from an advertisement and mushrooms from another print by Patricia Nimocks were assembled and glued to the box. A very light suggestion of grass was painted with acrylic using a sponge, and India ink lines and my name were drawn to help to unify all these diverse elements.

Then the traditional procedure, 15 coats of vinyl varnish topped with two coats of eggshell finish were used. Hardware was screwed in place; a lining was added; and the result is this purse by the author.

Uncolored Design Elements

This American black walnut and cherry lighter was handmade by Charles C. Burke. The prints come from a reprint book by Dover Books. The little figures were precisely cut and glued in this humorous arrangement. Note the little figure trapped on the top inside of the box.

The process was traditional using vinyl, then eggshell varnish.

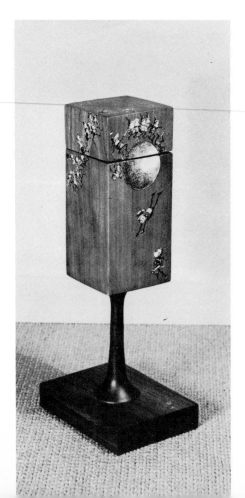

Result: A cigarette lighter or a conversation piece.

A fun wastepaper basket by Gini Merrill.

The top of a basket-purse by Lee Walker.

A table by Gini Merrill and Lydia Irwin.

A close-up of their table showing hand-painted borders, grass, and India inked poetry.

Little girl ballet figures dance around this purse by Lee Walker.

Another table with cutout and hand-lettered elements by Lydia Irwin.

A bookrack in an Americana theme by Lee Walker.

Mrs. Irwin's theme is almost always of floral or animal subject matter using hand-painted borders and lettering. This cabinet is not completed; the interior is to contain miniature three-dimensional animal scenes.

This corner cabinet resides in Lydia Irwin's kitchen. All the background is painted by hand and the sayings are lettered by Mrs. Irwin as well. The animals and flowers are cut out and glued in the traditional decoupage approach.

A decoupaged wardrobe by Fran Willner. The background is hand-painted and antiqued.

The inside of Mrs. Willner's wardrobe is even more fascinating than the outside. Designs are from prints and wrapping paper.

A stylized bird of peace on a gold-leafed plate by Dee Davis and Dee Frenkel.

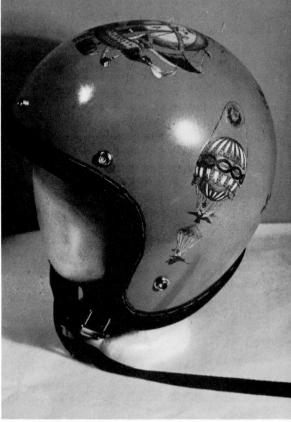

Transportation themes decorate this motorcyclist's helmet by the two Dees.

6

decoupage on glass and acrylic

One of the most popular and the quickest decoupage processes is working on transparent materials such as glass and acrylic and on reflecting materials such as mirrors. Decoupage is an attractive technique for decorating pictures, mirrors, lamps, glass-topped tables, plates, vases, and other glass containers and small parts such as switchplates. A heavy build-up of varnish is not necessary because most of the work is done in reverse.

This section describes gluing on glass and acrylic, making lamps with the use of pearly finishes, gessoing vases and other containers, and an unusual technique of using epoxy on crystal.

Gluing prints onto flat glass or acrylic is a bit easier than gluing on interiors of curved surfaces such as lamp cylinders and apothecary jars, but both require practice and patience. The best way to start is on a flat surface such as gluing a silhouette onto glass. But working with cutout designs is not particularly difficult. In some ways, it may be easier, because you can see through the transparent form to observe whether there are any air bubbles entrapped, whereas, in the reverse, you can only guess. Also the long, laborious varnishing and sanding sessions are eliminated because there is no need to heavily protect an internal surface that will have no wear and tear.

Using transparent colorants as background permits beautiful depths to color and attractive textures that are heightened when light transmits through the thickness of the glass and is particularly revealed when light travels between acrylic surfaces, as it is piped in acrylic.

Glass also can be used as a base and be rendered opaque with gesso and paint. This is particularly useful when the shape of the glass form is more important that its texture and color. An opaque covering can dramatize the importance of a form.

Perhaps one of the most dramatic results, though, is using epoxy as an adhesive and coating. It is a remarkable process because it is so easy, the product so attractive, and the time to accomplish this event so short. And the result is a very durable coating that can last forever.

Gluing Cutouts on Glass and Acrylic

Black and white and colored prints can be used. It is best to cut the prints into small units, but this one was not too difficult to handle, so I left it all in one piece. These are German silhouettes cut into very thin black paper. They are to be mounted on glass and framed. Glass from the frames is cleaned with alcohol to dissolve grease and fingermarks. Soap and water can also be used.

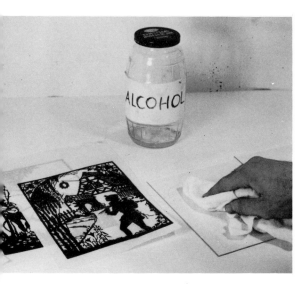

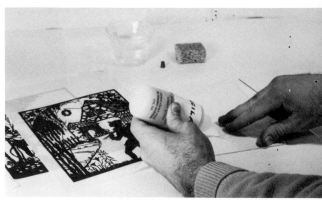

Mucilage (Harrower House) was used because it adheres well to glass. To slow the drying of the glue, you can add one-quarter teaspoon of glycerine to one-quarter cup of mucilage. Apply the glue to the glass and spread thinly with your fingers.

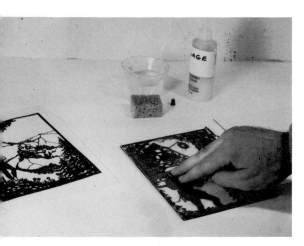

Place the picture face up on a piece of waxed paper. Then lift the waxed paper with print, and press it against the glass top first and then down to the bottom. Peel away the waxed paper. Press with fingers and sponge to make certain all pieces are completely adhered. Turn glass and print over to see whether air bubbles are trapped.

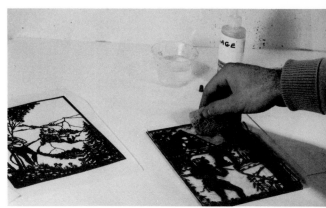

Clean away glue with sponge and water taking care not to disturb delicate sections. If stubborn glue spots remain, use a cotton swab and some warm vinegar and water to clean it away.

The completed pieces were backed with a pearlized Styrofoam "paper," the kind used as place mats on airline trays. It sticks to the glass without glue. And then, the pieces were framed.

Here acrylic emulsion is being brushed onto the surface of the mirror, for one strip at a time. The other sections are temporarily held in place only with putty.

Decoupage on Acrylic Mirror

Mirrors are now available from plastics suppliers in acrylic and can be cut to size with any saw. When the protective paper is peeled away from the mirror, it needs to be cleaned off with detergent and water. Since acrylic is the base material, acrylic emulsion is as good an adhesive as any. A milky-white at first, it dries to a clear transparent finish.

Coat the paper surfaces with four coats of acrylic emulsion, waiting for each to dry before applying the next coat.

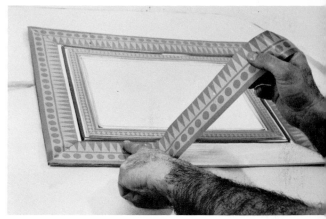

Wrapping paper was cut into strips with corners mitred to fit. To affix the paper, start at one end and work out bubbles with finger pressure as more and more of the strip is attached. Follow the same procedure all around, attaching colored paper strips and embossed gold stripping. For the gold stripping, add acrylic to both surfaces, the mirror and the back of the stripping, before fixing into place. Use a brayer lightly, if necessary, over the surface of the trim.

The mirror is framed in an aluminum do-it-yourself frame with Styrofoam sheeting glued with rubber cement to the back of the mirror to provide the one-inch depth required by the frame.

Decoupaging on Glass

A small carafe is cleansed of oil, grease, and dirt with soap and water and then denatured alcohol.

Spun Gold spray paint (Barrett Varnish Co.) is sprayed over the glass.

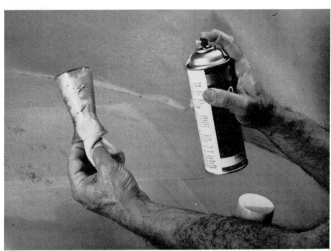

Then dry, gold-embossed forms are tacked in place and then glued with PVA. (See Chapter 2 for the preparation of these gold forms.)

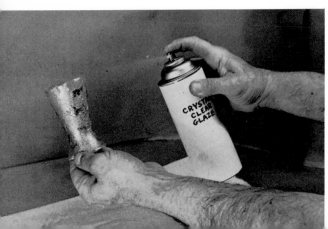

After the glue has set, crystal clear glaze (a glossy acrylic) is sprayed over the entire surface, with light applications, five times, until the surface appears glazed.

Carl Federer made this candy dish. Paper coins are glued onto the outside of the dish. A layer of opaque rust oil paint is applied over the entire form. When dry, black oil paint is painted over the rust color. Then more coins are pasted on so that they could be seen from the outside. The whole is glazed with varnish.

Barrett Spun Gold was sprayed on this plate and then paper shapes were glued over that pattern of gold. It was finished on the back with a clear glaze of acrylic. By Dee Davis and Dee Frenkel.

German embossed cutouts are trimmed and adjusted to fit onto this mirror. They are glued into place with mucilage. (See Chapter 2 for designing this mirror.)

When the glue has set, five coats of vinyl varnish are painted over the flowers and frame. Since the flowers are embossed, their relief quality is maintained by the minimum amount of varnish used.

Excess varnish and glue are cleaned away with cotton swabs dipped into turpentine.

The completed mirror certainly is enhanced with the bouquet decoration of flora.

Dee Davis and Dee Frenkel's "Venus" mirror. A cutout from a Botticelli reproduction is glued directly to the mirror.

Chinoiserie figures are applied to a dark red and gold frame with some shapes overlapping onto the mirror. By Fran Cohen.

Wrapping paper designs were cut from the background and arranged temporarily on the outside of this acrylic cylinder to test for matching and size.

Acrylic Cyclinders as Lamps

Acrylic cylinders are available in any number of diameters, thicknesses (gauges), and lengths. Any plastics supplier either stocks or can order these cylinders. They also are lightweight and for that reason, coupled with the fact that they are less apt to break, acrylic is a great material for lamp bases.

Since the paper was very thin, it was sprayed with sealer on the back only.

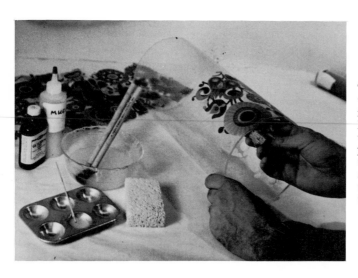

The cylinder was cleaned with cold-water detergent and water, to eliminate dirt and to retard static. Mucilage, mixed with a drop of glycerine, was used as an adhesive. But acrylic polymer emulsion would also be effective. Small units were glued, one at a time. Pressure was applied from the back while looking for bubbles through the outside of the cylinder.

After all the pieces were in place, a coating of acrylic was stippled with a sponge over the entire inside of the cylinder. This provided protection for the design and created a clear but textured coating.

Two coats of metallic pearl translucent finish with a gold patina (Liquid Pearl) were painted over everything, on the inside of the cylinder. The first coat had to be dry to the touch before the second coat was added. Any number of metallic finishes can be used, such as Treasure Jewels, and so on.

Since the metallic pearl lacquer coating was translucent, a layer of light orange acrylic was painted over that. It took a week for the metallic pearl to completely cure, free of odor, before the acrylic paint was added. Any number of color combinations and textures can be used. Try to pick colors that will complement your print. Various ways of applying metallic colors to the background will achieve different texture effects. You can streak the gold, dot it on, and so on.

There is a shallow but luminous depth to the background. This contrasts with the flat folk-art patterns used for this lamp. A wooden base and a burlap shade complete the picture. Lamp stores can provide the hardware attachments you need. Just bring in your cylinder for measurements.

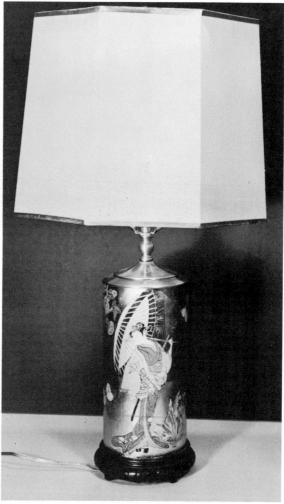

The background of this acrylic cylinder is gold leaf. Lamp by Gini Merrill.

Working on Glass

This lamp-to-be is in process. John Campbell and Lewis Morrow have cut and arranged flowers on a large vase in preparation for gluing.

A similar vase for a lamp by John Campbell and Lewis Morrow. The background is acrylic gesso. Cutouts are glued with mucilage.

Dolores Greig made this hurricane design that will become a lamp form. The glass was prepared by washing and drying. The design was glued on with Decal-It then the excess was cleaned off, sealed with two thin coats of acrylic spray, and five coats of acrylic gesso, as a background, each applied just after the gloss disappeared from the surface.

A completed lamp by John Campbell and Lewis Morrow.

This lamp by June Meier was stippled with Decal-It, coated with gold liquid pearl, and a final layer of turquoise acrylic.

The interior glass cylinder of this lamp by Dee Davis and Dee Frenkel was painted with gold oil paint thinned with turpentine.

Acrylic glaze (a sealer) is sprayed in a light coating over a clean liquor bottle.

Gesso Over Glass

Gesso can be used as a solid white background, its natural color, or as a blend of colors. Acrylic gesso and acrylic paint are compatible, so acrylic paint is an excellent colorant for gesso. Gesso sticks best over a spray-coating of clear acrylic, but can be applied to "raw" glass.

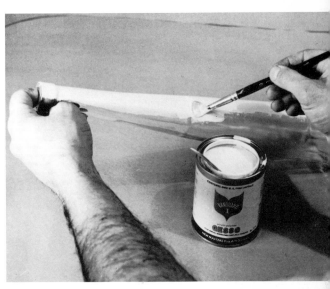

A coating of white acrylic gesso is brushed over the entire surface. When the coating has nearly dried (just lost its moist look), three more coats are applied, each one brushed in an opposite direction. (The bottom of the vase was not covered, because a piece of cork will be attached later.)

The final two coats of gesso are tinted light blue with acrylic paint . . .

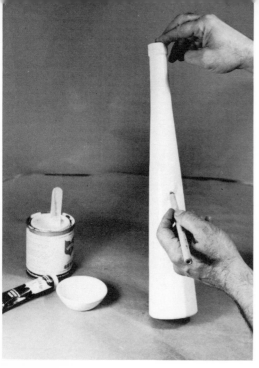

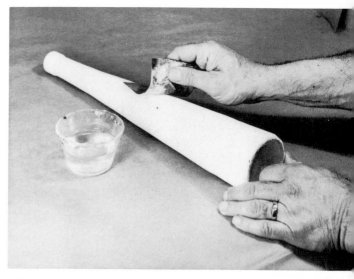

and brushed on in reverse directions.

When completely dry, the bottle is sanded smooth with #400 wet-or-dry sandpaper and water. At this point, the bottle is ready for decorations, cutouts, or in this case dried Japanese leaves.

PVA glue is used to adhere the leaves. It takes patience because some of the leaves' stems are stiff. After they are glued into place, the vase can be coated with a clear coating and considered complete. But in this case, I wanted to use an *Oshibana* technique. *Oshibana* is a contemporary Japanese paper collage art that uses natural materials and superimposed papers.

Dried, dyed leaves are temporarily arranged on the bottle.

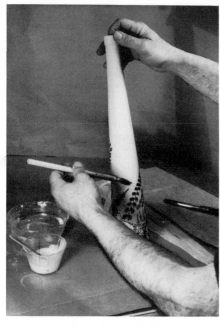

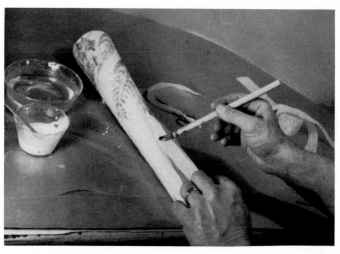

A coating of acrylic polymer emulsion is applied to the entire vase in preparation for a layer of white *Sakuragami* veil paper.

Cut to fit, the paper is attached to the vase and a coating of acrylic polymer emulsion is painted over it. This cuts down harsh colors with a subtle veil.

Another coating of acrylic emulsion is added, making certain that there are not any air bubbles entrapped.

The completed vase with ferns, flowers, and leaves over a very light blue background.

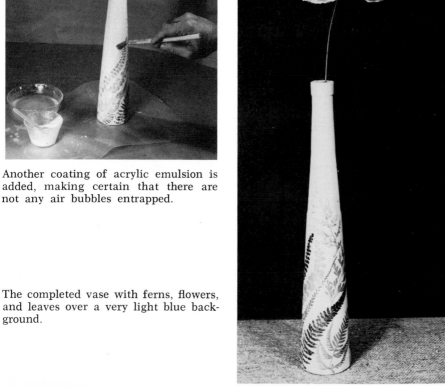

Nine coats of white gesso were applied to the outside of this old wine bottle, and when set, sanded smooth. Violets, butterflies, and a ribbon motif were applied in relief. Then the surface was varnished and pumiced. By Marie Mitchell.

A Japanese iris print in pink tones on rice paper is glued under glass and backed with a pink-yellow-green blend of gesso. Solid pigments of brown and green were pulled through the gesso at the base of the jar to create an earth effect. By Marie Mitchell.

137

Whimsical mice and mushroom prints are glued under glass and a soft background of gesso tinted with yellow ochre is added. By not mixing the color thoroughly into the gesso, a streaked texture was obtained. By Marie Mitchell.

A fragile Oriental print on rice paper is glued into the jar. A background of gesso tinted in pink complements the rust-red and white tones of the flowers. By Marie Mitchell.

Two metallic doilies, one gold and the other silver, are cut and reassembled to fit the Candlewick Crystal dish (by Imperial).

Equal parts of epoxy and catalyst are mixed together with a clean tongue depressor until thoroughly mixed.

When completely coated with epoxy, the crystal dish is placed over the doilies.

The whole—waxed paper, doilies, and dish—are turned upside down and the waxed paper is peeled away. Then with gloved hand, the doily is pressed firmly onto the dish, eliminating all air bubbles.

Epoxy on Glass

A two-part clear epoxy system is used as a coating and adhesive. Equal parts of epoxy are mixed and applied. It cures (dries) within a few hours to a very hard, glossy, water-clear surface with superb adhesion to glass.

The crystal plate is wiped with denatured alcohol to eliminate grease and dirt.

The doilies are placed right side up on a piece of waxed paper and a layer of epoxy is smeared over the entire surface.

Where the doily resists hand pressure, such as around the base rim, a tongue depressor completes the job.

By now the epoxy is hard. A fresh mixture of epoxy is readied and brushed over the entire surface on the back of the plate.

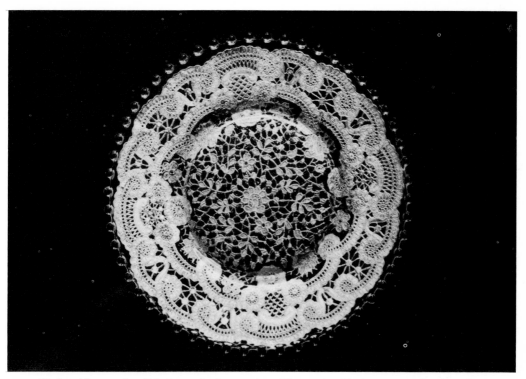

Right side up, the dish is ready for serving. The underside has a very hard surface.

Metal Foil on Glass

Wash and dry your glass form. Then paint mucilage over the entire surface. (You could use epoxy here, too.)

Immediately, wrap the bottle with aluminum foil. This is silver on one side and gold on the other.

Trim excess foil and press the remaining foil to the bottle.

Attach your design with more mucilage. In this case, they are figures of men in white, two shades of red-violet, red, and blue.

Varnish as you would any decoupage piece. After two coats, I rubbed some black acrylic into the indentations to dull the metallic shine a bit. Then I continued to varnish the surface until the figures were buried.

7

decoupage on ceramic, metal, cork, and papier-mâché

All materials can provide a base for decoupage. For some, imaginative license needs to be taken with traditional decoupage process.

Ceramic requires no special preparation except to make certain that the surface is clean, free of grease and dirt. Metal, after it has been prepared as suggested in Chapter 3, under "Preparation of Metal," is as simple as any traditional process. A new technique using epoxy that is immensely successful is described here. We have seen epoxy used with glass, but with metal as well as papier-mâché, it imparts a beautiful finish in a fraction of time. There are no problems with cork. Cork that is flexible, however, should not have too many coats of varnish.

Specific ways of working on these materials will be covered in pictures and captions.

Decoupage on Ceramics

Thin wrapping paper designs were used whose blues, violets, and red-violets blended with the royal blue stoneware bowl. They were cut, spray-sealed with a thin coating of acrylic, and glued with PVA to a clean bowl. Curves required adjusting by cutting thin pie slices into the shapes. Paper edges were touched up with acrylic paint. When the glue thoroughly dried, thin coatings of semi-gloss polyurethane were sprayed onto the bowl until eight coats in all were added. Each coat required overnight drying.

A fine #0000 steel wool was used to eliminate minor surface imperfections.

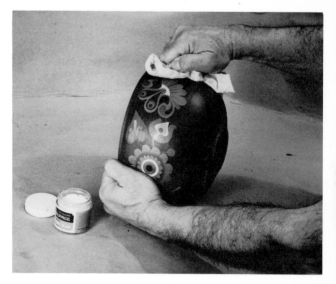

Finishing was completed with several coats of a mat wax applied with a damp cloth and then buffed with another clean, damp flannel cloth.

Urethane imparts a very hard, waterproof surface, not very different from the original stoneware itself. An alternate coating for this type of ceramic could be an eggshell finish. Both provide a functional and mat effect.

Twin porcelain perfume flasks by Carl Federer. Fine cutting of Renaissance prints and accents of embossed metallic gold trims were used. The entire piece was varnished with several coatings, enough to sink the prints.

Fran Cohen's ceramic vase boasts a very finely cut floral pattern. The entire piece was coated with at least 15 layers of varnish.

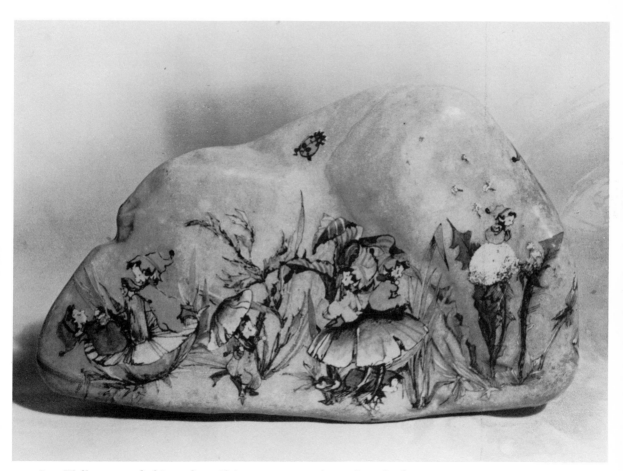

Lee Walker treated this rock as if it were a ceramic surface. In fact, it sports a glaze that is not too unlike ceramic. Elfin figures dance around the rock. The process is traditional decoupage, except that the rock needs to be washed, scrubbed, dried, and sealed with an acrylic sealer before figures are added.

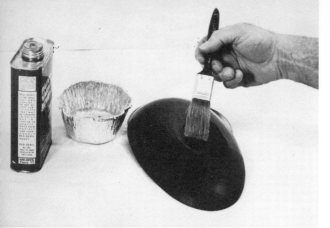

Paint remover is being brushed onto this cast-iron dish to remove the old finish.

Decoupage on Metal

Refer back to Chapter 3 for specifics on treating metal. Be certain of two things before decoupaging: First, that the metal will not rust and second, that the finish will not flake away. Trays, wastepaper baskets, lamps, tables, and bowls are some of the many metal forms conducive to decoupaging.

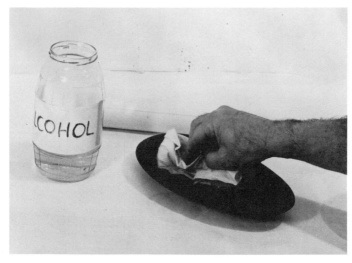

The paint and remover were scraped away and now the dish is cleaned with alcohol. Next, a rust-preventative black paint is brushed on.

Figures are cut from an old Chinese print. Two-part clear epoxy is mixed and then brushed onto the backs of the figures in preparation for gluing.

146

One unit at a time, they are pressed into place with a plastic-gloved hand, making certain that no air bubbles are trapped between paper cutout and dish.

There is no need to wait for the epoxy adhesive to completely cure. As soon as it has set, a second batch of the same crystal clear epoxy is mixed together and this time brushed in flowing strokes over the entire surface of the iron dish.

The result is a porcelain-like finish with no distortion of the print and complete protection for the metal surface. There is no need to sand the finish because there are no air bubbles or imperfections.

In keeping with the design of this copper mug, a nautical theme was selected. A finely cut clipper ship was glued into place with mucilage. (PVA glue is an alternative adhesive).

When the mucilage was completely dry, the entire mug was coated with eight applications of vinyl varnish.

When the varnish dried, the entire piece was sanded with steel wool (#oooo). Steel wool works better when there are indentations in a surface, as the convolutions of this copper mug.

The final copper mug with black and white engraving.

This metal tray was decoupaged in the traditional process by Carl Federer.

Another tray by Carl Federer with a colorful snake, butterflies, and jewels on a gold metallic background.

Lydia Irwin's porch candle lamp with a decoupaged background and hand-painted details.

A collage tray where various picture elements are superimposed on a black metal tray. By Carl Federer.

Decoupage on Cork

Unless cork is supported with a rigid background, as in the project with an ice bucket, take care to limit the number of vinyl coats to be used. Cork can be colored with acrylic paint; two coats are advisable. Some coats of vinyl or urethane varnish will make your piece more waterproof and stain resistant. Cork boxes, containers, place mats, and coasters are some of the items that make excellent backgrounds for decoupage.

Once, this bare cork ice bucket "cried out" for decoration. A nautical theme suggested by the cork and the shape was used. The cork was cleaned of grease, wax, and dirt and then the pieces (by Patricia Nimocks) were glued into place with PVA. Slomons Quik glue was used to adhere a rope trim.

The final piece has a few coatings of urethane.

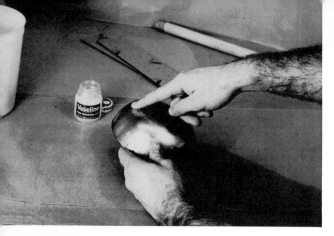

PAPIER-MÂCHÉ AND DECOUPAGE

Making forms of papier-mâché is a natural background for further applications of paper cutouts. Two approaches, both very different, are detailed here.

Making a Papier-Mâché Bowl

A mold is coated with petroleum jelly to act as a separator. All materials are gathered: a container for mixing the Décomâché with water, two guides for the dowel "rolling pin," waxed paper, and a pizza cutter.

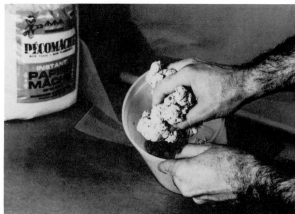

The Décomâché, a prepared papier-mâché mix, is kneaded with water to a workable consistency.

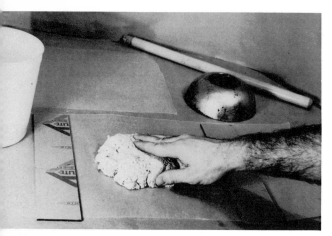

On a piece of waxed paper, the papier-mâché mixture is centered between two of the same thickness guides that will determine the future thickness of the bowl.

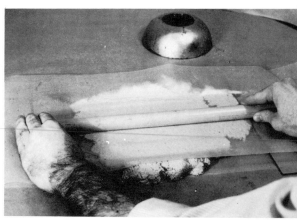

Waxed paper is then placed over the lump. Using a piece of old broom handle as a rolling pin, the mix is flattened out by rolling the dowel over it, taking care not to allow any of the papier-mâché to squeeze over onto the guides. Otherwise, the piece will not end up being the same thickness throughout.

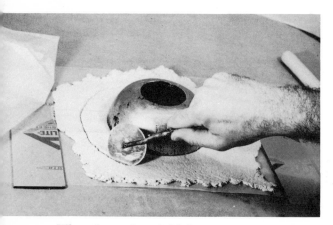

When the papier-mâché flattens to an even sheet, a pizza cutter is used to outline the diameter and demarcate a circle, enough to cover the mold. A knife can be used but it tends to pull and lump the mix.

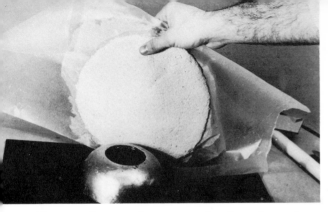

The waxed paper that was under the mix, and circle of papier-mâché, are positioned over the coated mold.

The circle is then formed via hand pressure around the coated male mold. A female mold form would also work, but, as with the male form, with no undercuts, else the dried paper form would lock into place and not be removable without destroying it.

When completely dry, usually in 24 to 36 hours, the papier-mâché bowl is lifted from the mold. Note that there is no warping if the form is allowed to dry completely.

Some sanding and filing may be necessary to finish the edges and outside surface. If the mâché mix was properly formed, the inside surface should be an exact duplicate of the mold.

The petroleum jelly is cleaned away with alcohol.

Acrylic modeling paste is used to plug up any imperfections, followed with five coats of acrylic gesso, inside and outside.

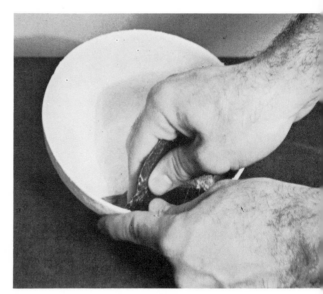

When the gesso is dry, wet-sand the bowl smooth with #400 sandpaper. The outside was allowed to remain somewhat rough to keep the papier-mâché mix quality.

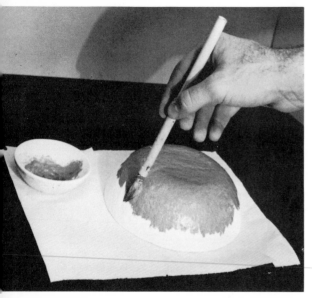

Then dust the bowl with tack cloth and paint it with acrylic paint. The outside was painted vermillion and the inside was left a natural gesso white.

Edges are touched up with acrylic paint after the design has been cut and glued in place. (See Chapter 2 on the planning of this design.)

A two-part crystal clear epoxy system was mixed in equal parts and with spatula, the whole interior of the bowl was generously covered. The outside was coated with two coats of vinyl.

This epoxy surface is as beautiful as porcelain, thick enough to sink or bury the paper cutout with one application. No sanding was necessary because the surface was smooth and clear.

A papier-mâché decoupage plate, discovered in a London flea market. Late 19th century.

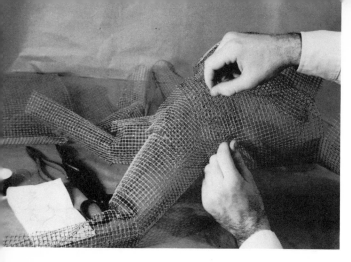

Making a Papier-Mâché Figure

Carpenter's cloth was used as the basic framework for *Maxima Minnie* (note sketch). Pieces were sewn together with wire.

The skeleton assembled, paddings of paper were stuffed into place.

The basic contours formed and taped into place, *Maxima Minnie* was ready for papier-mâchéing.

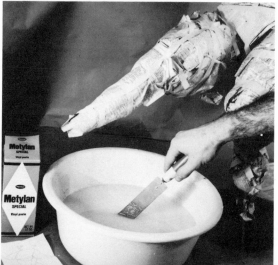

Metylan, a vinyl paste used for paper hanging, was mixed according to recommended proportions with water and stirred. Wheat paste can also be used.

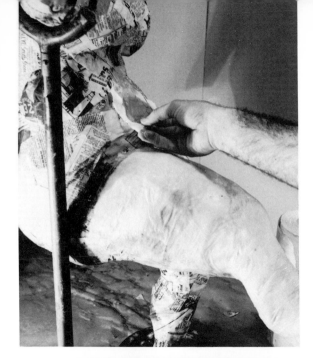

Four complete layers of overlapping newspaper strips and Metylan are topped with two finishing layers of paper toweling and the paste mixture. Hint: if you want edges of paper to blend, always tear paper into strips, never use a scissors or paper cutter. Note that paper has a grain and will tear into longer strips in one direction than the other.

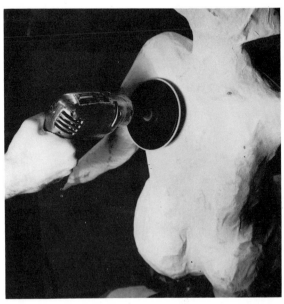

When completely dry, high spots were sanded away and then areas that required patching were patched with acrylic modeling paste, if small, or more papier-mâché, if larger.

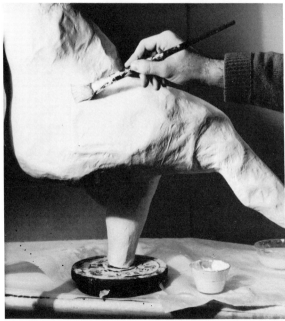

Minor imperfections were filled, then when dry, three coats of acrylic gesso were applied followed by a final coating of peachy-pink acrylic paint.

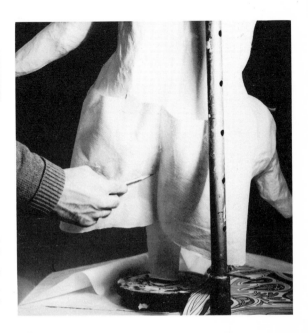

When the paint dried, flexible paper toweling was attached and a pattern for her mini bathing suit was sketched. Using the pattern, her bathing suit was cut from a colored paper poster, other areas from colored paper, and decorations were made of Mylar rickrack and metallic trim. All attachments were adhered, decoupage style. Then the whole piece was given three coats of a "fun" finish.

To anchor her into a base, a polyethylene basin was sprayed with a silicone release agent in preparation for a pouring of polyester resin (even though polyethylene is a natural release agent).

Polyester clear casting resin was colored blue and then the prescribed amount of catalyst was added. All parts were mixed together thoroughly.

Maxima Minnie was positioned with the leg that was to bear her weight in the basin and the catalyzed polyester was poured into the basin around her leg.

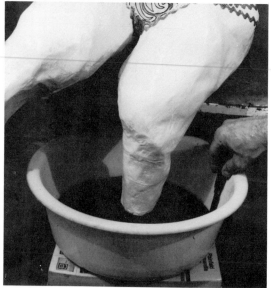

When cured (about two hours) a knife was inserted around the edge to release the now solid base from the basin and *Maxima Minnie* was removed.

Here she is in all her glory, foot deep in water, ready to take a plunge.

8

decoupage in relief

Three-dimensional decoupage has been variously named and widely interpreted. Some consider a *vue d'optique* arrangement of paper cutouts that project from a background a decoupage technique. I don't. It is a paper art and fun to do, but has nothing to do with varnishing and other decoupage finishing processes. In *vue d'optique*, several prints are cut up and superimposed at shallow depths to simulate perspective. A valid papercraft, it belongs to papercraft as does collage.

Relief decoupage employs cutouts in relief, or repoussé, or as Marie Mitchell calls it *moulage*. Whatever name used, it is decoupage in relief much like a bas-relief. Prints are sculptured and shaped onto the object and buried under varnish. To accomplish this sculptured effect, elements are stuffed with a moldable and supporting mastic-like substance, attached to a flat background and then varnished. Some design elements in the background can remain flat, while others project in a shallow relief.

Some subjects lend themselves more easily to sculpturing in relief than others. Remember that the design element is made of paper and that paper can stretch just slightly. Figures, cherubs, flowers, butterflies, animals, and birds are some good relief subjects.

Modeling of these figures is possible within limits. Parts of a form that are nearest project more, such as arms, heads, breasts, and there are indentations, for example, in a figure, around the arms, underneath the chin, at the waistline, in drapery folds. Features of a head can follow general cavities and projections, for eye sockets, under the nose and lips, and to distinguish the hairline. How this is accomplished is detailed in the projects that follow.

The supporting or mastic material to be used can vary from French clay (a powdered porcelain-fine unfired ceramic clay) mixed with PVA, to RTV silicone, and one (that I do not prefer), ground up tissues mixed with mucilage. One other technique is to use a cornstarch clay and mix it according to the directions on the cornstarch box. Another, is to substitute instant papier-mâché for the mastic, and still a different approach is to mold a wet print on the reverse side over a piece of Styrofoam with a tool, pressing areas that are to project for a repoussé effect. Paper mixtures tend to shrink.

An example of *vue d'optique* by Lee Walker in a watermarked taffeta-covered box with velvet trim. Leaves are sculptured in relief. A ceramic plaque is in the center. Clear acrylic sheet encloses the composition.

Relief with French Clay and PVA

Cut out and prepare your print by spraying it face side *only* with an acrylic sealer such as Krylon or Blair. The back part should not be sprayed because it has to remain soft.

Prepare the French clay by mixing two tablespoons of French clay (a powder) with one teaspoon of PVA (Elmer's or the like) and one-quarter teaspoon of water. Knead the clay mixture like bread dough. If it sticks to your fingers you used too much water. Add a bit more French clay. Cover the mixture with plastic to keep it from drying out. Mix only what you need for the particular project that you are working on.

Gini Merrill is mixing Elmer's Glue into French clay.

She has just added water and is stirring the mixture.

Next comes kneading the doughlike material and shaping a small amount into the general outline of the subject to be in relief.

Mrs. Merrill then coats the back of her print with PVA.

She adds the kneaded clay-dough to the center of the print leaving a tiny margin all around. Leftover clay can be stored for a short time if wrapped in waxed paper.

Gini Merrill attaches the piece to her unvarnished purse lid.

With her fingers, she gently presses and shapes the pelican form and fixes it to the lid.

A sculpturing-burnishing tool is used to further refine the pelican in relief, by pressing where indentations should go; the clay pushes out into the areas that should project more. Edges are gently pressed down with the burnisher.

With a cloth dipped into clear water, she cleans away excess clay that may have seeped out.

The completed purse, fully varnished and sanded. By Gini Merrill.

Relief on a rock requires a very clean rock. Sand, wash, and scrub away all dirt and loose particles. Let the rock dry.

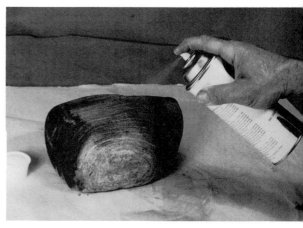

Seal the rock's surface with an acrylic sealer.

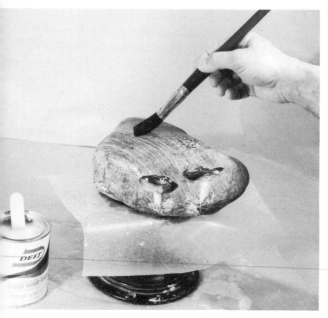

Apply the relief and flat forms as demonstrated in Gini Merrill's project. When dry, varnish. Deft, a lacquer-based finish, was used here. It should be flowed onto the surface.

When dry and sanded in the usual approach, mask an outline around the base and paint or spray rubber cement on the surface.

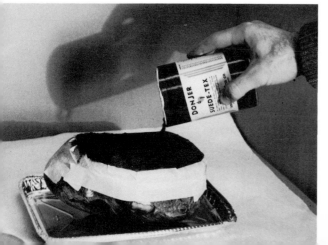

To protect table surfaces from heavy-rock scratches, sprinkle a flocking (Donjer's Suede-Tex) over the fresh rubber cement. In a half-hour, shake off excess flocking. Repeat the operation if necessary.

The completed rock with a tiny frog leaping over the mushrooms.

A basket purse by Gini Merrill with animals in relief and flowers left flat in the background.

Mrs. Merrill painted some elements, lettered the Thackeray saying, glued flat cutouts, and placed her leopard in relief—all on a parchment shade.

Sylvia Simon's interpretation of relief using a tissue (Kleenex) and PVA mixture.

Another purse with animals by Gini Merrill.

The scene is flat but the figures of Sylvia Simon's purse are in relief.

Dolores Greig made this box placing mushrooms in relief.

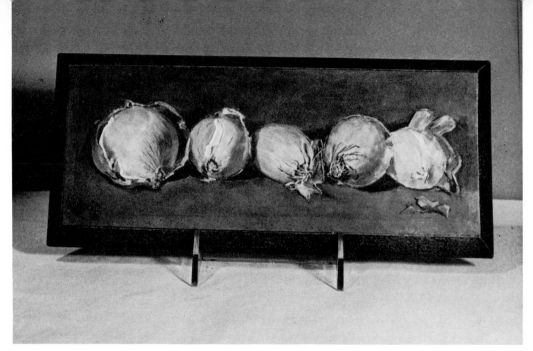

Using a cornstarch filler and two prints, superimposed, Lee Walker created this lovely composition of onions.

This octagonal box, designed and executed by Marie Mitchell in the Hiram Manning Studio, has a Venetian green background. The prints were hand-colored in shades of blue and violet. Angels are in relief using ground-up tissues mixed with PVA.

The design for this chest was composed from three French prints that were hand-colored with pastels. The background is antique white, and the interior lined in gold velvet; only the figures are in relief. Door and drawer knobs are gold-plated. By Marie Mitchell.

Relief with RTV Silicone

A pocketbook that was covered in brown suede (See Chapter 4) has two slide-out wooden panels that can alternate as design. This panel was painted with a sky-blue acrylic paint. Japanese veil paper was adhered with PVA to the background to create cloud effects.

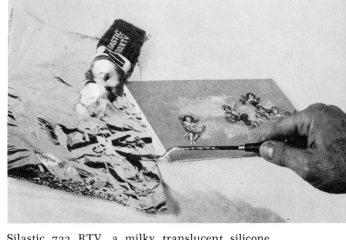

Silastic 732 RTV, a milky translucent silicone that is moldable and dries hard, was applied to the backs of the angels so that the angels, which are embossed shapes, will stand away from the background.

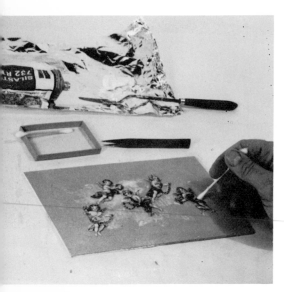

With a cotton swab, excess was cleaned away. The RTV silicone acts as an adhesive as well as a filler for the relief.

The completed panel is lined to match the purse lining and slid into place.

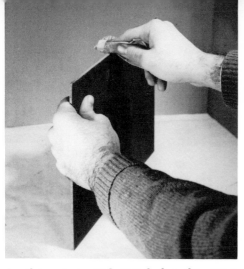

Another raw wood panel for the same purse was coated with gesso, sanded, and a red-orange coating of acrylic was brushed on. The edge was sanded so that it would slide smoothly into the grooves of the pocketbook.

Vinyl was brushed over the acrylic, and gold leafing applied. A gold-leafing brush was used to smooth the leafing.

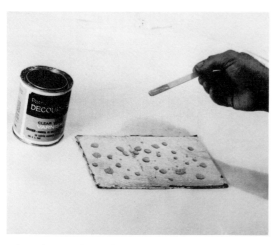

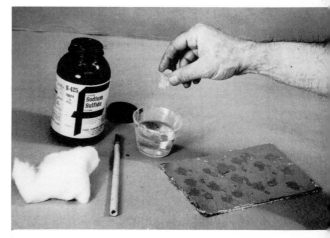

After the vinyl dried, spots of vinyl varnish were scattered randomly over the gold-leafed surface.

When the vinyl spots dried (they acted as a resist or preserver for the original gold color), about one-half teaspoon of sodium sulfide crystals was dissolved into a half cup of water. It is a smelly concoction.

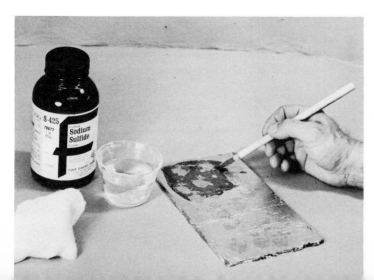

The solution was brushed over the gold leafing and the discoloration was immediate.

171

The longer the sodium sulfide solution is left on, the darker it gets. Meanwhile, variations of color can be achieved by blotting off the mixture with water-saturated absorbent cotton.

A series of seven stars are cut from the original and then stacked one on top of the other with RTV silicone. Smaller center pieces are glued around the large star with PVA. When dry, the whole panel was varnished with vinyl, until at least ten coats were applied and the smaller stars were buried.

After sanding and waxing, the completed panel, in golds and golden browns, was lined with the same lining material of the box and was inserted in the brown suede purse. The original box shape is by Lok-Box, Inc.

9

cut paper decoupage

Some of the most exciting and creative designs can be achieved with cut paper. There are no limitations and no need to search for prints. If you have an idea, you can cut it from paper and then process it as in traditional decoupage.

Various textures of paper can be used, from construction paper to exotic handmade papers and hand-painted varieties. The design elements are your individual creation. Certainly, the result is unique.

One point to remember is that you must seal your papers to keep colors from bleeding and running when glued and varnished.

In this chapter, a range of contemporary design possibilities on a variety of objects is explored.

Probably the most simple approach is cutting paper silhouettes which are nothing more than the outline of a shape. Sometimes,

parallel incisions and patterns are cut out from within the form to define significant detail such as the round pollen area in the center of a flower, or the veins in a leaf. Just about any subject can provide inspiration for a silhouette form. This kind of design has a folk art quality, perhaps because it has been widely employed in folk art forms. You have the advantage of creating a unique design that is not very difficult to carry off.

Another variation of paper cutting is cutting of outlines and combining it with paper folding. The result can be as simple as repeating paper dolls to more complex *mon-kiri*, which is paper folding and cutting to produce crests. Single crests can be made from various folds to borders and repeated designs. Your hand and scissors provide the magic.

The exploded design idea, developed in

detail in Chapter 2, is another approach. All these simplify a form to its essential shape—its outline and internal detail. Each is another style that distinguishes one paper cutting idea from the other. So you can explore with paper from a traditional folk art, or traditional Oriental base with *mon-kiri* to very abstract forms in the exploded design.

Let us not exclude free paper cutting using juxtaposed paper shapes. Here too, the design can be formal as in the "impossible" figure, or completely free as in the "tour de force" table. The same kind of paper can be used, or great variety in texture and pattern can interplay in the design. The inspiration can come from simple or complex geometric shapes, to stylized subjects breaking details down into planes, areas, and patterns, or to completely non-objective shapes with no connecting natural world subject matter orientation. This technique is not too different from collage, except that shapes are juxtaposed and not overlapped. (Although you can also overlap.) The choice is yours.

Cut Paper in Silhouette

The possibilities of this silhouette design in cut paper were explored in Chapter 2. After the design was sealed and glued into place, it was varnished with 15 coats of vinyl varnish and then with two final coats of eggshell varnish to impart a mat surface.

Cut Paper in an Exploded Design

This large raw-tinware deed box by Burkart was cleaned with alcohol to remove its protective film.

The entire box was painted with rust preventative black enamel paint.

Using a handmade Japanese paper, a design is sketched onto the surface. (See the development of the design in Chapter 2.)

Following penciled outlines, the paper is cut into patterns.

The design is refined and "exploded" by spreading or expanding its elements.

Its central unifying grid is attached.

Two views, front and back, before adjustment of the paper to fit the form.

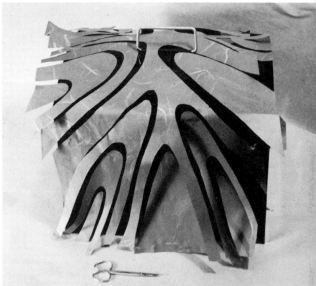

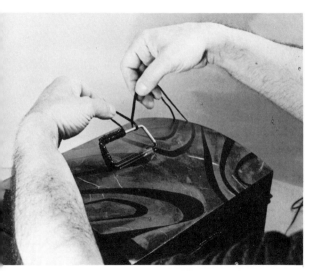

The paper was adhered with PVA and the whole varnished with McCloskey's Be-Tween-Kote which acts as a sealer and adhesive bond for dissimilar kinds of materials. It is only used as a sandwich coat between enamels and phenolics, oil-based paint and vinyls, etc. In this case the varnish in service was Fuller O'Brien Pen-Chrome, which is an alkyd-phenolic. After many coats were applied, the whole piece was sanded and waxed. Then a lacing stitch covered the raw metal handle.

The former raw-tin deed box is now a traveling case for cosmetics and what-nots.

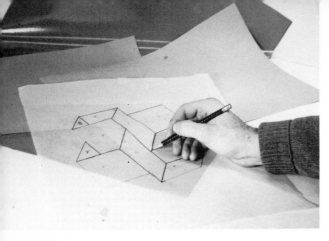

Cut Paper in an "Impossible" Figure

Inspired by a Josef Albers drawing, an "impossible figure" design is created. Colors are earmarked on tracing paper, and on the appropriate sheet of thin construction paper (Reycote) the shapes are traced with pencil.

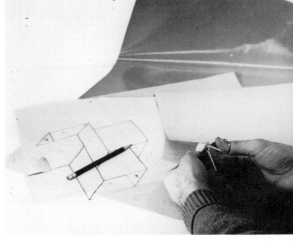

Each color is cut and placed on the original pattern.

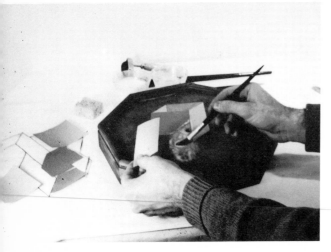

On an acrylic-stained wooden clock base by Dek Company, the pieces are glued with PVA, following the model on the left.

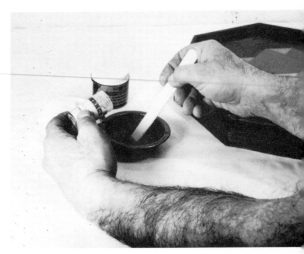

After varnishing with seven coats of urethane until the thin paper was buried, it was sanded, and then pumice and linseed oil were mixed together.

With a flannel (or felt) padding, the mixture is rubbed on the surface, then wiped away, producing a beautiful, smooth finish.

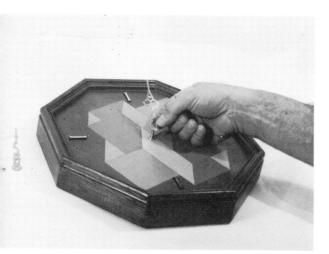

A battery attachment, numeral, and hands are attached.

An incongruous design becomes the face of an octagonal clock.

Cut Paper in a *Mon-kiri* Design with Mother-of-Pearl

A Japanese papercutting art called *mon-kiri* or crest making has a long history. Japan's Samurai, the warriors of yesteryear, took great pride in the decorations that appeared on their armor and banners. The design each warrior adopted became his family crest.

Squares of paper are folded in half diagonally and then into two, three, four, five, or six folds. Then an outline is drawn on the final fold and the whole cut out. Experiments in drawings can create all kinds of designs. The one shown here is a difficult five-fold called the "cherry blossom."

Start with a square of paper, the size to suit your object.

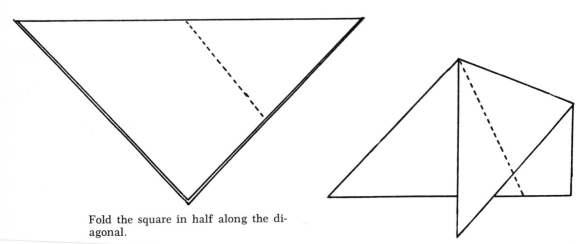

Fold the square in half along the diagonal.

Then starting from the midpoint of the diagonal, fold down a flap at a 36° angle. Fold that side again at a 60° angle. Crease the edges sharply with the back of your fingernail.

Next, fold the opposite side back along the edge and you should have a five-fold shape that looks like the next figure.

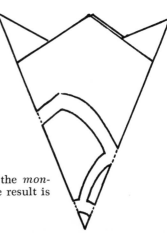

Draw an area to be maintained as the *mon-kiri* design and cut away excess. The result is a crest when the paper is unfolded.

The paper *mon-kiri* ornament is spray-sealed and glued onto the box with PVA. Mother-of-pearl is placed over the areas to be inset with it and an outline is traced with pencil.

Boiling hot water is placed in a dish and the mother-of-pearl is soaked for ten minutes, enough to make it pliable.

The leaf of pearl is removed with tweezers and with a decoupage scissors the pencil outlines are cut.

PVA is applied to the back of the leaf and glued to the surface. If the leaf loses its luster after gluing, do not worry, it will return after varnishing. A mat varnish was used in the traditional mode. The whole was rubbed with #ooo steel wool to a smooth surface.

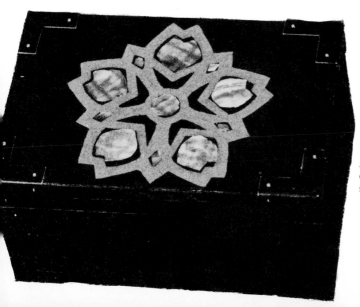

After waxing, the mother-of-pearl luster comes alive. *Mon-kiri* can be a very personal and effective design source.

Three views of the Geoff Jones table.

A Tour de Force with Cut Paper

This creative result was a contrapuntal relationship between two minds. I had commissioned Geoff Jones, a woodworker, to make a hutch-chair-table of pine (with oak feet and braces) and with some design modifications—such as eliminating the "Colonial" trimmings. I told artist Jane Bearman of an idea to make a figure of a child in flat paper sitting on the chair side. Jane thought of the "Queen of 'Arts" idea since the table was to become a game table. Since it was her idea, Jane Bearman designed and executed that section in her own image. I planned and made the top of the table. The result is . . .

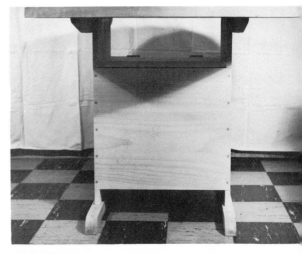

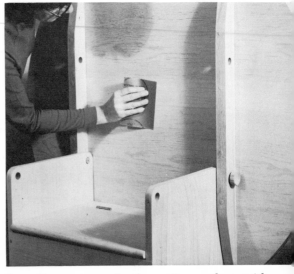

Jane Bearman sands the entire surface with #320 wet-or-dry sandpaper.

She dilutes epoxy varnish, two-thirds varnish to one-third distilled turpentine, into a sealer . . .

and coats the entire table with it.

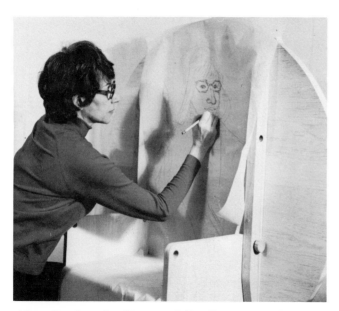

After drawing the "Queen of 'Arts" image as her own self-portrait, Jane Bearman transfers it to the seat.

Jane darkens the tracing lines.

A close-up of Jane's self-portrait.

She then cuts some basic shapes to fit patterns she had traced, and glues them into place.

Each piece closely juxtaposes the next in precise arrangement. Note that the bench lid is unattached at this point.

Jane Bearman fitting a piece into place. Note her inspiration nearby—a queen of hearts card.

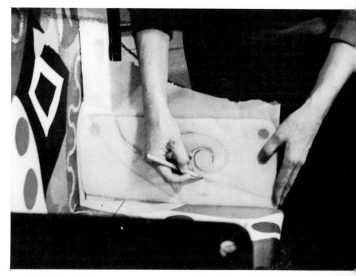

A tracing is made of a side piece to fit the area.

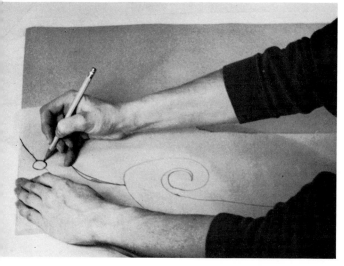

It is then transferred to the colored glazed paper . . .

and is glued into place with PVA.

The tabletop is painted with black acrylic, as are sides and ballet slipper feet. The interior storage box was done in orange and red. And the top is arranged in multiples of multicolor paper squares in a chessboard design with embossed metallic pre-cut forms surrounding it. These were glued into place with PVA and the entire piece was coated with 15 layers of urethane (Varathane). At two intervals, the entire piece was electric- and hand-sanded. After waxing, the surface is almost indestructible.

A close-up of the top.

A close-up of one side.

The remarkable "Queen of 'Arts," by Jane Bearman.

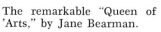

10

some "exotic" techniques

Sometimes a difficult shape such as a ball or egg will impose problems, such as how to attach a flat piece to it without forming wrinkles, but when solutions are worked out, these discoveries lead to a whole new avenue of expression. Such is the case with fragmentation, a technique of fitting flat surfaces onto curved forms. It could be a serious technique as expressed by Carl Federer, or a fun approach as explored here.

Another "exotic" is the technique of *trompe l'oeil,* a fool-the-eye method of making the unreal, flat piece actually look as if it is the real thing. It is a piece of technical trickery not to be confused with realism. Some painters used trompe l'oeil techniques to exaggerate an effect. There can be a pop art quality to this process as well. Using today's vernacular, looking at some pieces done in the trompe l'oeil approach can "blow

your mind." It certainly means to surprise and shock.

Plastics can provide some surprises in approach, too. Working on and with plastics has been explored throughout the book. Certainly almost all the varnishes and glues used were plastics. Except when an acrylic mirror or lamp base was used, most plastics were employed as a means to an end, but here we see plastics used as an end in itself, in three very different processes.

Fragmentation

Have you ever tried to attach a flat picture onto a curve? If you have, you know that, for the piece to lie flat on the curve, you have to make slits and cut out pie-shaped pieces for the flat piece to fit, often destroying the integrity of the original. Fragmentation maintains the essence of the design, although it does eliminate pieces, but it does so in thin slivers, so thin that the continuity of the form is not lost. Fragmentation is the cutting of a picture into thin parallel strips, sometimes straight, sometimes curved. The result often looks like contour farming flattened out. Pieces fit very closely. The whole is then varnished.

Trompe l'oeil is great fun because it starts out as a witty idea and is created with a twinkle in the eye. The end result is a harmless "practical joke" that, incidentally, takes a good deal of thought and skill to carry out.

Whereas trompe l'oeil has roots in tradition, plastics and equivalent techniques that utilize plastics' potential do not. In fact, the best use of plastics is to deny history and to allow plastics to suggest their own processes. That is what happened in using the acrylic polyhedron. I could have applied an opaque shape and material but the object would have lost some of its essence—a play of light within and from without the form. I decided, therefore, to use a translucent paper, a transparent colorant (watercolor), and a transparent adhesive-coating. The result was successful, inasmuch as light still works within the shape while mirroring the paper-color image.

Transferring a print also uses transparency. The opaque paper behind the print was removed, leaving just the ink attached to a transparent plastic coating that was applied to the ink surface. Plastic, then substituted for the opaque paper and when attached to the transparent acrylic cylinder it became one and the same—an integral part of the vase.

Polyester resin makes paper transparent by penetrating the fibers of the paper so that light can be transmitted from front to back. Polyester preserves paper this way; instead of remaining a coating on paper the polyester impregnates the paper, becoming polyester-paper. Epoxy does not penetrate, it remains a surface coating even though the surface quality appears very much the same. Although only one project with polyester is shown, the range of possibility is tremendous. When fiberglass is combined, for instance, three-dimensional forms can be made that have their own strength and need no alternative supports. Tables, chairs, lamps, boats, trays, and sculptures can be made this way. The technique is the same as working with papier-mâché. Instead of paper, use fiberglass cloth or mat, and instead of wheat paste and water, use polyester and catalyst. Apply it the same way. Finishing is the same, except that color is mixed directly into the resin rather than painted on top (but you can also paint on top of polyester). For details about mixing polyester, look ahead in this chapter, as well as the approach to making *Maxima Minnie* in Chapter 7. She could have been made with fiberglass. Note that her foot is embedded in polyester resin that became the base.

In the end, I hope that you enjoy exploring processes and expanding your design vocabulary. Release from what has come before and what someone else has done can lead to fulfillment. Bringing into being an object that you alone were responsible for creating is one of the most rewarding experiences one can have!

A Styrofoam egg is used for this project; but any kind of egg, real, ceramic, or plastic, can be used. A large nail is inserted into the base to provide a "handle." Acrylic modeling paste is smoothed over the entire surface, two to three times, until the foam texture is completely covered.

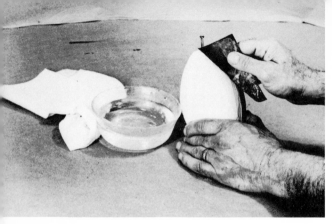

Rough areas are wet-sanded smooth with #400 sandpaper. Two coats of acrylic gesso are applied and also sanded.

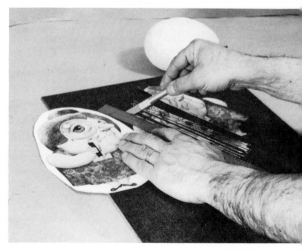

The illustration, taken from a Dixon-American Crayon Company advertisement, is spray-sealed. Using a steel ruler and a sharp knife, part of the design is cut into thin straight parallel strips with the picture sequence maintained. (Stay away from fans, because this could be a difficult puzzle to put together.)

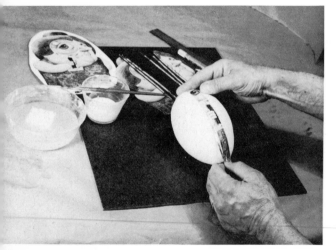

Strip by strip, the pieces are glued into place, juxtaposed very closely together. Wherever pieces do not fit, they are either eliminated or adjusted with knife or decoupage scissors.

Some areas are cut into contours following the curves of the design. For this kind of cutting, I used a swivel cutter with a rotating blade, that easily traversed around curves (see foreground).

A piece of paper towel roll is covered with the bottom part of our "Prang lady" and will act as a base. All parts are varnished and finished as in decoupage. (Waxed paper is used to protect surfaces.)

Imperiously, our lady looks through her magnifying glass-monocle. She is somewhat reduced from her original bulk, but very much the same person. Fragmentation is one way for a body to lose some weight.

A small egg (hen-sized) covered in the fragmentation process with a Renaissance lady. By Carl Federer.

Trompe l'oeil

Trompe l'oeil takes some painting skill in addition to decoupage technique. You have to stimulate depth on your two-dimensional surface cutting pieces, considering perspective lines, and then paint in depth lines and shadows following rules of perspective. Also light should hit at a consistent point and shadows fall in their natural place. It might be wise to practice lighting a composition to see where light and shadow fall and how they drape over contours. Then degrees of light and dark need to be reproduced using the base color of your object in the darkness of the area being painted. For instance, if the book is a light green, then light green should be included in the gray-blacks of your shadows.

Book jackets and pictures representing sculptures from book jackets were used to simulate a bookcase in this two-drawer white cabinet. Pieces are measured, arranged, rearranged, planned for color distribution, and cut with perspective lines in mind. Pieces were eliminated and added in order to create a convincing arrangement.

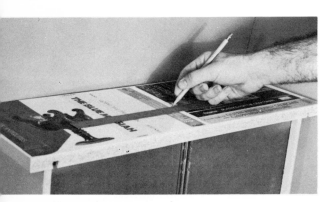

All the pieces are glued into place with PVA. Then perspective lines are drawn, indicating a depth to the bookshelf.

General background areas are painted in with degrees of gray to black, as light and shadow would fall in a bookshelf.

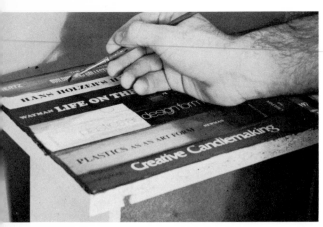

More subtle shadows are painted with acrylic paint suggesting the roundness of the back of a book. Colors are coordinated with the overall color of the book jackets. Shadows of the sculptures and other books are also painted on.

The entire piece was sprayed with acrylic sealer and then an alkyd-phenolic varnish was used in the traditional approach. The final test was to ask someone to fetch a book from "that bookcase." One dented hand later we heard the reply, "#%&*)!!!."

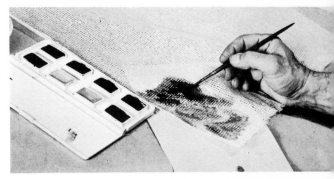

Solid Acrylic and Acrylic Glaze as Adhesive and Coating

A patterned web of Japanese handmade paper was colored with water colors in a nonobjective design.

A solid, clear acrylic 14-sided polyhedron, to be exact, a quadra-decahedron, is placed over the design to see how and where colors should be placed. It seemed that five sides should be covered, allowing these colors to be mirrored and magnified within the polyhedron through reflection and refraction.

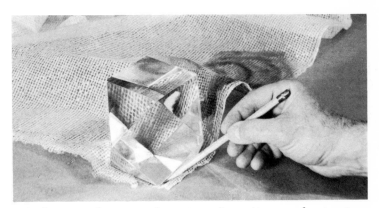

Outlines are drawn on the water color patterns and cut out.

An acrylic crystal clear glaze was sprayed under and over the paper. The acrylic glaze acted as an adhesive and coating. Six more light coats were added. After the first spraying, the sides not to be covered were cleaned of spray and then masked with masking tape to eliminate the need for further cleaning. I would advise you to mask the piece first, before spraying.

The acrylic spray glaze acted as an effective coating. Note the way the colors are reflected and refracted. Moving this piece is an entertainment as the internal illusions change.

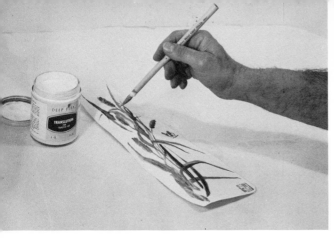

Transfer from a Print

Here is a fascinating modification of decoupage, the art of lifting printing inks from paper and transferring them to wood, metal, or, in this case, an acrylic cylinder.

Acrylic polymer emulsion can be used for this technique, but I used Deep Flex Translution because it is a bit thicker in consistency and the results are obtained with fewer coats. Brush four coats of the emulsion over the front of the print all the way to the edges, each in a different direction, allowing each coat to dry before applying the next. Each coat takes about 30 minutes to dry and when it does it turns from milky to clear. Allow the piece to dry overnight. Clean your brush with water.

Mix Deep Flex's PRS Concentrate in one gallon of warm water. This helps cut surface resistance and is optional. Then pour it into a flat container, large enough for your print to lie flat. Submerge your print for three or more hours, even overnight.

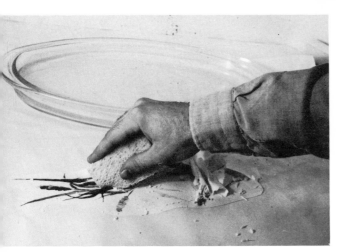

Remove your print from the water. The coating on the face will look cloudy but will clear up later. Peel off the paper from the back. Use a sponge or your fingers to roll off the rest of the paper. Finer pieces come off if you gently rotate your fingers over the paper specks. Keep your print wet with clear water while you remove the paper.

After all the paper backing has been removed, cut away excess plastic just as you would cut away excess paper. The material is flexible and limp, but not at all difficult to cut.

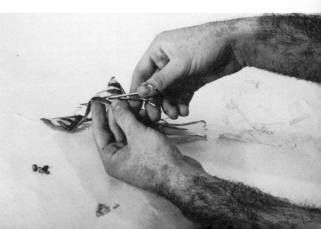

Meanwhile, ready the object you are to transfer your print to—in this case, an acrylic cylinder that will become a vase. Clean the acrylic with methyl alcohol.

Apply a coating of the same polymer to the acrylic or whatever you are using for the transfer base.

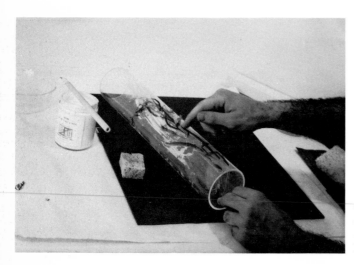

Then lay the cut print down on the emulsion and press out excess emulsion and air bubbles just as if you were pasting a paper print.

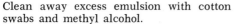

Clean away excess emulsion with cotton swabs and methyl alcohol.

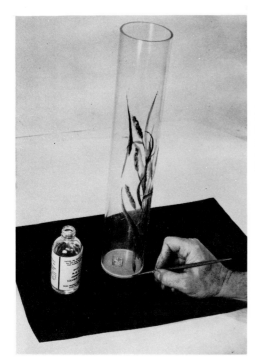

At this point, I attached an acrylic disc to the base to form the vase. Just sit the cylinder on the base and with a brush run methylene chloride (G.C.35) around the seam. The solvent will seep into the crack by capillary action and in a few moments the cylinder vase is complete.

The completed wheat print on the vase with the real thing in it.

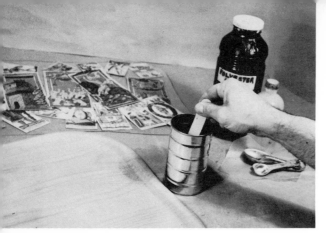

Mix polyester resin and the manufacturer's indicated amount of catalyst together in a clean, dry can. Try not to introduce air bubbles as you thoroughly stir both ingredients together.

A Polyester Embedment

Polyester resin tends to penetrate paper and make it transparent, so it is quite important that only those images that complement a design should be on the back of your paper. Except for that quality, polyester resin is a fine material to use to sink a print on a flat surface. To counteract the transparent effect, use a non-oil- or non-wax-based metallic paint on the back. Epoxy, which works similarly to polyester resin, works best on curves because it is more thixotropic (will not drain down to the bottom so quickly).

Any clear laminating or clear casting resin will work. The process should be carried out in a 70°F dry room. Curing time is about an hour, depending on how heavily the resin is catalyzed. Keep fingerprints off of the surface for at least 24 hours. Because of a gaslike odor, keep your areas well ventilated.

Pour the catalyzed mixture on your clean, dust-free, grease-free, dry surface. (The finish was removed from this tray in preparation for pouring.) Save a bit of resin for another pouring.

Spread the resin over the surface evenly. Make certain that your surface is level.

Dipping each design in under the resin, so that both top and bottom are coated, place your pieces in position.

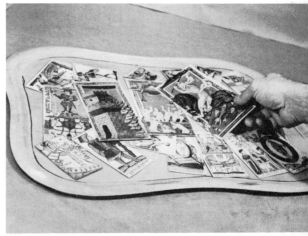

Make certain all pieces are properly positioned before the resin cures. They sometimes float around. Otherwise, it is too late to modify your design after the resin cures.

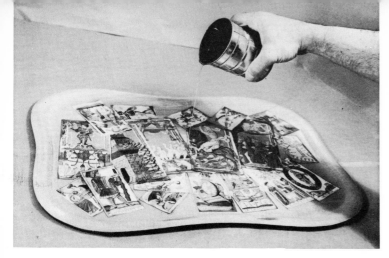

Before the resin gels, pour additional resin over the top of the design.

With a tongue depressor or a spatula, continue to distribute the resin until all of the paper and tray is covered and no air bubbles are apparent. No bubbles should be trapped under the prints.

Place a piece of Mylar over the entire tray pressing the covering down from one end so that *no* air bubbles become trapped underneath. The Mylar cover is not essential, but it does provide a tack-free, smoother surface.

After the resin cures, pull away the Mylar.

The completed tray with old picture cards. Note that some have become transparent, but do not seem to interfere with the design.

Construction Collage

Boxes are secured with a cloth-backed adhesive tape to create a three-dimensional construction. Then photographs, prints, colored paper, poems —anything of any theme—can be cut, fitted, and glued to the sides of the boxes. Each construction should have its own theme. The entire piece is varnished decoupage-fashion and finished with sanding and waxing.

This construction on a "Pursuit of Happiness" theme is by Barbara Schwartz.

bibliography

HARROWER, DOROTHY. *Decoupage, A Limitless World in Decoration.* New York: Bonanza Books, 1968.

KENNY, CARLA AND JOHN. *Design in Papier-Mâché.* Philadelphia: Chilton Book Company, 1971.

MANNING, HIRAM. *Manning on Decoupage.* New York: Hearthside Press, Inc., 1969.

MEILACH, DONA Z. *Papier-Mâché Artistry.* New York: Crown Publishers, 1971.

MITCHELL, MARIE. "The Art of Decoupage." Instruction manual, Detroit: Marie Mitchell Decoupage Center, 1970.

———. "Advanced Decoupage." Instruction Manual, Detroit: Marie Mitchell Decoupage Center, 1971.

MOSELEY, SPENCER; JOHNSON, PAULINE; AND KOENIG, HAZEL. *Crafts Design.* Belmont, California: Wadsworth Publishing Co., 1963.

NEWMAN, JAY HARTLEY AND SCOTT, LEE. *Plastics for the Craftsman.* New York: Crown Publishers, 1972.

NEWMAN, THELMA R. *Plastics as Design Form.* Philadelphia: Chilton Book Company, 1972.

———. *Plastics as an Art Form.* Rev. ed. Philadelphia: Chilton Book Company, 1969.

NICKERSON, MAYO. *Oshibana.* New York: Takashimaya, 1965.

NIMOCKS, PATRICIA. *Decoupage.* New York: Charles Scribner's Sons, 1968.

O'NEIL, ISABEL. *The Art of the Painted Finish.* New York: William Morrow & Co., 1971.

RÖTTGER, ERNST. *Creative Paper Craft.* London: B. T. Batsford, Ltd., 1970.

RUBI, CHRISTIAN. *Cut Paper Silhouettes and Stencils.* New York: Van Nostrand Reinhold Co., 1970.

SEITZ, WILLIAM C. *The Art of Assemblage.* New York: The Museum of Modern Art, 1961.

SOMMER, ELYSE. *Decoupage Old and New.* New York: Watson-Guptill Publications, 1971.

WING, FRANCES S. *The Complete Book of Decoupage.* New York: Coward-McCann, Inc., 1970.

supply sources

The following sources will help you get started. If you have an arts and crafts store nearby, chances are that they will carry a complete line of decoupage supplies.

Boxes and Other Objects

Burkart Bros., Inc.
6th Street and Highland Avenue
Verplanck, N.Y. 10596
Metal objects

Carson and Ellis
1153 Warwick Avenue
Warwick, R.I. 02888
Unpainted tole and tinware

Colonial Handcraft Trays
Newmarket, Va. 22844
Bare metal trays

Davis Lynch Glass Company
P.O. Box 4286
Star City, W.Va. 26501
Hurricane globes

Dek Company
Box 1314
Amarillo, Tex. 79105
Boxes, frames, plaques, clock frames, and parts

Griffith-Bateson
Betty and Geoff Jones
Box 49, Pine Street
S. Walpole, Mass. 02071
Furniture-makers, tables, chairs

Houston Art and Frame
2520 Drexel Drive
Houston, Tex. 77027
Plaques, boxes, frames

J & R Industries
P.O. Box 4221
Shawnee Mission, Kan. 66202
Picture frames, boxes, plaques

Lok-Box, Inc.
Boxwood Lane, R.D. 9
York, Pa. 17402
Panel boxes, redwood boxes, panels

Morris Manufacturing Company, Inc.
3837 Dividend Street
Garland, Tex. 75040
Boxes, frames, plaques

Wicker World
20651 Mack Avenue
Grosse Pointe Woods, Mich. 48236
Baskets

Colorings: Paints and Special Finishes

Barrett Varnish Company
1532 South 50th Street
Cicero, Ill. 60650
Exotic spray paints such as Spun Gold

Connoisseur Studios, Inc.
Box 7187
Louisville, Ky. 40207
Liquid Pearl and Treasure Gold

American Art Clay Company, Inc.
4010 West 96 Street
Indianapolis, Ind. 46268
Easy Leaf, synthetic gold leafing, Rub 'n
Buff

The American Crayon Company
(Dixon)
Sandusky, Ohio 44870
Prang acrylic paint

Hunt Manufacturing Company
1405 Locust Street
Philadelphia, Pa. 19102
Vanguard acrylic paints, emulsion and modeling pastes

Permanent Pigments
27000 Highland Avenue
Cincinnati, Ohio 45212
Liquitex acrylic paints, emulsions and modeling paste

Decorative Trims

Available at all general suppliers plus
these specialists:

Walbead, Inc.
38 West 37 Street
New York, N.Y. 10018
Embossed decoupage decorations

William E. Wright Company
West Warren, Mass. 01092
Self-adhering Stick-to-Trims

General Decoupage Suppliers

Dick Blick
P.O. Box 1267
Galesburg, Ill. 61401

Boin Arts and Crafts
91 Morris Street
Morristown, N.J. 07960
and:
75 South Palm Avenue
Sarasota, Fla. 33577

Connoisseur Studio
Box 7187
Louisville, Ky, 40207

Cunningham Arts Products, Inc.
1564 McCurdy Drive
Stone Mountain, Ga. 30083

Economy Handicrafts
47-11 Francis Lewis Boulevard
Flushing, N.Y. 11363

Hazel Pearson Handicrafts
4128 Temple City Boulevard
Rosemead, Calif. 91770

Marie Mitchell's Decoupage Center
16111 Mack Avenue
Detroit, Mich. 48224

Houston Art and Frame
2520 Drexel Drive
Houston, Tex. 77027

Model Craft Hobbies
314 Fifth Avenue
New York, N.Y. 10001

The O-P Craft Company, Inc.
425 Warren Street
Sandusky, Ohio 44870

Sax Arts & Crafts
207 North Milwaukee Street
Milwaukee, Wisconsin 53202

Supreme Handicrafts
P.O. Box 395
Sioux Falls, S.Dak. 57101

Hardware and Accessories

Angelo Bros. Co.
2333 North Mascher Street
Philadelphia, Pa. 19133
Lamp parts

Houston Art and Frame
2520 Drexel Drive
Houston, Tex. 77027
Hinges, handles, catches, glides

J & R Industries
P.O. Box 4221
Shawnee Mission, Kans. 66202
Hinges, handles, screws, catches, wire, cast
metal ornaments

Lok-Box, Inc.
Boxwood Lane R.D. 9
York, Pa. 17402
Hinges, handles, catches etc.

Morris Manufacturing Company
3837 Dividend
Garland, Tex. 75042
Hinges, handles, catches etc.

Lamp Products
P.O. Box 34
Elma, N.Y. 14059
Lamp parts

Acrylic Cubes, Cylinders, Mirror, Sheeting

Ain Plastics
65 Fourth Avenue
New York, N.Y. 10003

Industrial Plastics
324 Canal Street
New York, N.Y. 10013

Studio Plastique
W. H. Glover, Inc.
171 First Avenue
Atlantic Highlands, N.J. 07716

Adhesives

Harrower House of Decoupage
River Road
Upper Black Eddy
Bucks County, Pa. 18972
Mucilage for decoupage

Miracle Adhesive Corp.
Bellmore, N.Y. 11710
Water clear epoxy

Slomons Lab, Inc.
32-45 Hunters Point Avenue
Long Island City, N.Y. 11101
Sobo and Quik

3M Company
St. Paul, Minn. 55119
3M Spra-ment rubber cement

Adhesive and Non-Adhesive Linings

W.F.R. Rebbox Corp.
583 Avenue of the Americas
New York, N.Y. 10011
Crushed velvet, burlap, velour

Temporary Adhesive

Brooks Manufacturing Company
1051 Meredith Drive
Cincinnati, Ohio 45231
Plasti-Tak

Cork

Bayonne Millwork & Lumber Company
Broadway at 17th Street
Bayonne, N.J. 07002
All kinds of cork

Equipment

J. L. Hammett Co.
2393 Vaux Hall Road
Union, N.J. 07083
Swivel cutter #5039

Skil Corp.
5033 Elston Avenue
Chicago, Ill. 60630
Dual Action Sander #490

Flocking

Donjer Products Company
1398 Utica Avenue
Brooklyn, N.Y. 11203

Papier-Mâché Mixes and Adhesives

Riverside Paper Corp.
Appleton, Wisc. 54911
Décomâché

Henkel, Inc.
Teaneck, N.J. 07666
Metylan paste

RTV Silicone

Dow Corning Corp.
Midland, Mich. 48640
Silastic 732 RTV

Transfer Emulsions

Connoisseur Studios, Inc.
Louisville, Ky. 40207
Decal-It

Deep Flex
Box 11471
Fort Worth, Tex. 76110
Translution and PRS Concentrate

Prints and Other Design Sources

Andrews-Nelson-Whitehead
7 Laight Street
New York, N.Y. 10013
Exotic papers imported from all over the world

Brandon Memorabilia, Inc.
3 West 30 Street
New York, N.Y. 10016
New and old embossed prints, trims, wide assortment of unusual and old prints

Connoisseur Studies, Inc.
Louisville, Ky. 40207

Designs Galore by Lee Walker
5174 Lakeshore Road
Port Huron, Mich. 48060

Dover Publications, Inc.
180 Varick Street
New York, N.Y. 10014
Dover coloring books

Foster Art Service Inc.
430 West 6th Street
Tustin, Calif. 92680
Soft cover art books, prints, etc.

Varnishes

Deft
Torrance, Calif. 90503

Pierce & Stevens Chemical Corp.
Box 1092
Buffalo, N.Y. 14240
Fabuloy

O-P Craft
Sandusky, Ohio 44870
Flair Finish

Cunningham Arts Products, Inc.
1564 McCurdy Drive
Stone Mountain, Ga. 30083
Flourish

The O'Brien Corp.
Baltimore, Md. 21213
Fuller-O'Brien Pen-Chrome

American Handicrafts Company
Fort Worth, Tex. 76110
Hallmark

McCloskey's Varnishes
Philadelphia, Pa. 19136
McCloskey's Heirloom

Brocado, Inc.
2451 S. Ashland Avenue
Chicago, Ill. 60608
Mod Podge

Miracle Adhesives Corp.
Bellmore, N.Y. 11710
Miracle Epoxy

Connoisseur Studios, Inc.
Louisville, Ky. 40207
Patricia Nimocks Decoupage

New York Bronze Powder Company
519 Dowd Avenue
Elizabeth, N.J. 07201
Polyurethane Spray

Cunningham Art Products Inc.
Stone Mountain, Ga. 30083
Royale Coat Decoupage Finish

Sapolin Paints
201 East 42 Street
N.Y., N.Y. 10017
Sapolin Polyurethane Clear Coating

The Flecto Company Inc.
Oakland, Calif.
Flecto Varathane Satin

Waterlox Chemical and Coating Corp.
Cleveland, Ohio 44105
WaterLox

glossary

Abstract art. An artist's private way of seeing the world, by emphasizing, distorting, eliminating elements of the real world to suit the idea.

Analagous colors. Colors that sit side by side on the color wheel, e.g., red-violet, violet, and blue-violet.

Arte povero. Italian for decoupage, literally meaning "poor man's art."

Assemblage. All the paste-up arts and also three-demensional arts that employ dissimilar elements in a composition. Collage, decoupage, and montage are some examples of assemblage.

Brayer. Rubber coated roller used to distribute glue and press out air bubbles.

Bridges. The temporary thin paper attachment that supports thin elements and keeps them from tearing away; later cut away before pasting.

Carpenter's cloth. A metal mesh used as a base for papier-mâché.

Chinoiserie. Use of Chinese motif in 18th-century design.

Collage. The pasting and gluing of papers, fabrics, and any kind of material into a composition.

Complementary colors. Opposites on the color wheel, e.g., red and green, yellow and purple, blue and orange.

Contour. The outline of a shape. The outside edge.

Decoupage. The employment of reproductions or paper forms as cutouts, which are pasted, varnished, and sanded until the original decoration is completely embedded.

Design means. Elements we employ relating to space—such as color, line. How we express ourselves; the symbols we employ, such as textures, color, line, planes, shapes and balance of shapes, and darks and lights in a given space.

En grisaille. French term for a predominantly gray monochrome palette reminiscent of marble sculpture. Sometimes used with turquoise blue, terracotta, and opaque white.

Flocking. A finely macerated wool or cloth used as a protective base, often for the underside of an object to keep it from scratching another surface.

Fragmentation. Attaching of a flat image to curved surfaces by cutting the picture into thin strips before pasting.

French clay. A dry white or light gray powdery material much like ceramic clay before water is added. Used with water or PVA to provide the filler for repoussé.

Gesso (acrylic). A painting ground or base that acts as a sealer and painting surface for colorants. It can also be mixed with acrylic paint to form a thick colorant.

Glue for decoupage. A water-soluble, transparent, non-staining adhesive that will stick to anything; usually polyvinyl acetate or polyvinyl chloride.

Gold leaf. A form of exceedingly thin foil 4-5 millionths of an inch thick made of pure or synthetic gold used in gilding.

Japanning. A term used in England to describe decoupage.

Lacche povero. See *arte povero.*

L'art scriban. French for decoupage.

Mat varnish. Varnish usually containing wax, pulverized mica, and talc to reduce luster.

Mon-kiri. A Japanese paper folding and cutting art usually used to create crests.

Monochromatic colors. A single color and variations of that color dominates.

Montage. In two-dimensional art, it is the overlapping of pictorial elements, usually two-dimensional.

Mother-of-pearl. A hard, iridescent inner substance of shells such as that of the pearl oyster. Used as accents in decoupage.

Moulage. Another word for repoussé with paper to create a bas-relief.

Non-objective art. Pure design elements used to express an artist's ideas and feelings without any direct reference to the real world.

Oshibana. A contemporary Japanese paper collage art that uses natural materials and superimposed papers.

Photomontage. The use of photos or reproductions of photos in a composition that utilizes the overlapping and superimposition of these elements.

PVA. Polyvinyl acetate. See Glue for decoupage.

Repoussé. A shallow relief much like bas-relief that shapes the material so that it projects away from a base.

Representational art. Subject matter that faithfully represents the subject.

Rhus vernicifers. Lacquers of the 18th century, imported from China and Japan, that were made from the sap of the *rhus vernicifers* tree.

Rottenstone. A powdery substance somewhat like pumice stone, made from decomposed siliceous limestone; used mainly for polishing.

RTV (silicone). Room temperature vulcanizing, rubber-like material, sometimes silicone. Used in decoupage as an adhesive-filler for repoussé.

Sakuragami. Veil paper. A translucent, thin handmade paper usually in different textures made in Japan.

Sealer. Usually a plastic spray or diluted shellac used to protect a print or close the pores or grain of an object.

Sink a print (bury a print). Application of enough coatings of varnish, with commensurate sandings, in order to completely embed the print in the varnish.

Tack cloth. A resinous varnish cheesecloth with a waxy feeling that picks up dust.

Thinning a print. Peeling away excess paper backing of a print.

Transfer of a print. Lifting of printing inks from paper and transferring them to another surface by means of acrylic-type coatings.

Triadic colors. Colors equidistant on the color wheel, e.g., red, yellow, blue.

Trims. Usually gold and silver embossed foils as well as any other decorations that are used to define an area or accent some part of the design.

Trompe l'oeil. A fool-the-eye method of making the unreal, flat piece actually look as if it is the real thing. A piece of technical trickery, not to be confused with realism.

Varnish. The overall term that covers transparent coatings and that includes lacquers as well.

index

Italic numbers indicate illustrations